VGM Opportunities Series

OPPORTUNITIES IN
ELECTRONICS
CAREERS

Mark Rowh

Foreword by
Dick Glass
President, Electronic Technicians Association

VGM Career Horizons
NTC/Contemporary Publishing Group

Library of Congress Cataloging-in-Publication Data

Rowh, Mark.
  Opportunities in electronics careers / Mark Rowh. Foreword by
    Dick Glass. — Rev. ed.
        p.   cm. — (VGM opportunities series)
    Includes bibliographical references (p.   ).
    ISBN 0-8442-1841-3 (c). — ISBN 0-8442-1845-6 (p)
      1. Electronics—Vocational guidance.   I. Title.   II. Series.
  TK7845.R68   1999
  621.381'023—dc21   98-42440
                                                                  CIP

Cover Photo Credits:
Images copyright © 1997 PhotoDisc, Inc.

Published by VGM Career Horizons
A division of NTC/Contemporary Publishing Group, Inc.
4255 West Touhy Avenue, Lincolnwood (Chicago), Illinois 60646-1975 U.S.A.
Printed in the United States of America
International Standard Book Number: 0-8442-1841-3 (cloth)
                                     0-8442-1845-6 (paper)

  ⁀⁀ 00 01 02 03 04 LB 18 17 16 15 14 13 12 11 10 9   8   7   6   5   4   3   2

DEDICATION

This book is dedicated to Bill Burns, Jim O'Hara,
and technical wizards everywhere.

CONTENTS

ABOUT THE AUTHOR

Mark Rowh is a widely published writer as well as an experienced educator in community college and vocational-technical education. He serves on the administrative staff at New River Community College in Dublin, Virginia, and has also held administrative positions at Greenville (South Carolina) Technical College and at Bluefield State College and Parkersburg Community College in West Virginia.

Rowh holds a doctorate in vocational and technical education from Clemson University, and he has worked closely with a variety of technical programs in his career as a professional educator.

Rowh's articles on educational and career topics have appeared in a wide range of magazines. He has contributed several other books to the VGM Career Horizons series.

FOREWORD

A CAREER ON THE LEADING EDGE—
ELECTRONICS

You may have a thousand career choices, but not many give you the chance to work with the smallest element in the universe—the atom and its electrons—with the most exciting consumer electronics products, or with space-age communications. In this field you will understand basic electronics, actually working with calculations that prove that an amp of electrical current is $6.24 \times 1\ 01\ 8$ electrons flowing past a point. You will learn that radio-TV-satellite transmissions travel at the speed of light, 186,000 mps, and that this is useful to technicians in their work in radio-TV, satellite, radar, and other areas.

The information superhighway is here. It is here because electronics technicians installed it, assist engineers in designing the products required by it, and keep it working for the benefit of mankind. Without this most important individual, the world would be a much less efficient place, still using smoke signals or tin cans connected by a string, or hollering across the ravine in order to communicate. As you can see, electronics technicians have very exciting careers.

You may not find it easy to be a part of all of the segments of the electronics industry at the same time, but fortunately you can choose to be a part of those that will reward you for your time and expertise and that are so interesting that you can't wait to go to work each day. Here are some of the exciting areas that the Electronics Technicians Association offers certification in: fiber optics installation; consumer electronics; satellite communications; master antenna signal distribution; computer service; computer network service and installation; cellular, paging, and telephony services; biomedical equipment; industrial electronics, including robotics and computer numerical and programmable controls; avionics; global positioning systems; home automation and security; military fire control and communications; and many areas of wireless communications.

Is special training required? You bet. If you have average ability in math and physics, like a little chemistry, like to work with your hands, use test equipment and can diagnose electronics and communications problems, you can study to become an electronics technician. You will learn how components such as transistors and integrated circuits work together in an electronics product. You will understand the operation of these high-tech modern-day miracles, and you will enjoy the rewards of bringing them on-line or back up to original operating levels. You will achieve a sense of accomplishment each day.

As you advance in your understanding and abilities, you will have numerous opportunities to step up to higher paying positions, to work with the newest technologies, or even to start your own business. Few other careers offer you so much. Few other careers are as exciting. One of the nice parts about entering the electronics profession is that you can choose to study and work in a segment of it that does not require intensive and extensive study and years of training, such as cable or fiber optics installation, or you can complete an education that puts you at or above the education levels of professionals in many engineering jobs. You get to choose the best and most enjoyable career slot for you.

Electronics isn't for those who slept through high school classes or who shied away from courses that required thinking: physics, geometry, algebra, computers, or math. It isn't for the lazy or for those who dread challenges. It is for those who want to utilize their mental and physical powers to the fullest. If that is you, welcome to the ranks of the world's electronics technicians—those who keep the high-tech world turning.

Dick Glass, CETsr, EHF
President, Electronics Technicians
Association, International

ACKNOWLEDGMENTS

The author greatly appreciates the cooperation of the following in the researching and writing of this book:

American Electronics Association
Edison Community College
Electronics Technicians Association
Haywood Community College
Howard Community College
Institute of Electrical and Electronics Engineers
International Society of Certified Electronics Technicians
New River Community College
U.S. Department of Labor

INTRODUCTION

Hey, nobody said choosing a career is easy! After all, occupational choices are among the most important decisions anyone makes. These decisions should be made carefully and thoughtfully. You need to consider a variety of factors. We all know that decisions rendered today can shape your life for years to come.

So, have you considered a career in electronics? This is one occupational area in which technological change provides great potential for men and women with the appropriate interests and aptitudes. Unlike many job areas that become displaced by advancing technology, electronics remains at the forefront of such change. This means that if you choose an electronics career and obtain the right training, chances are excellent that this background (combined with continuing education in years ahead) will serve you well in the decades to come.

For any reader interested in electronics, this book is offered as an overview of the basic facts needed in considering and planning ahead for a career in this field. The material offered here should provide any interested person with a basic understanding of this challenging occupational area.

CHAPTER 1

THE PROMISE OF ELECTRONICS

Electronic devices are everywhere. Take a minute and consider just how wide-ranging the impact of electronics technology is on everyone's life today. For example, in the last week have you:

- watched television?
- operated a computer?
- used a portable or desktop calculator?
- driven or ridden in an automobile?
- used a microwave oven?
- watched a videotape?
- used an automatic teller machine?
- listened to a radio or compact disc player?
- checked the time with a digital watch or clock?

All of these functions, and many others too numerous to name, would be impossible without electronic components. Thanks to the many marvelous capabilities provided by electronics technology, hundreds of conveniences are made possible in the home, school, workplace, and elsewhere.

Think about how you spend the first few hours of an ordinary day. You get up at a preset time, thanks to a clock-radio that offers a variety of electronic functions. You may prepare breakfast with a microwave oven, watch the morning news on television, and then ride to school or work in an automobile or bus that depends on computerized controls to start the engine and keep it running. During the morning, you may use a computer yourself or interact with someone else who does. If you visit a store or restaurant, the checkout process probably will depend on an electronic cash register. Ditto for any banking activities. Any information you receive—whether from radio, television, newspapers, or textbooks—will have been transmitted, printed, or processed with electronic equipment. At any time, day or night, your life is enhanced by the practical applications of electronics.

Electronic devices don't just provide convenience. They also promote health, safety, and other serious matters. For example, hospitals use a variety of electronic devices in helping patients by diagnosing and treating illnesses. The military services, as has been so vividly demonstrated in televised reports of modern warfare, have been revolutionized by "smart" bombs, cruise missiles that can travel hundreds of miles with pinpoint precision, and other weapons based on advanced electronics.

Thanks to the growing role that electronic devices play in virtually all aspects of modern society, careers in electronics represent one of the most promising of all areas of employment. The ability to work with electronics is a valuable skill.

Persons who can design, build, install, or repair electronic devices or components hold a wide range of interesting jobs.

A career in electronics can entail anything from working in an assembly line or making simple electronic components to helping design a complex piece of high-tech equipment. In many instances, the work performed will be the repair of existing items rather than the development of new ones.

Whatever the tasks involved, working with electronics requires special knowledge and skills. As a result, women and men who have acquired these capabilities often find themselves in an advantageous position when it comes to seeking good jobs and pursuing challenging careers.

ELECTRONICS VERSUS ELECTRICITY

Before reviewing the subject of electronics further, it is important to make a distinction between careers in *electricity* and those in *electronics*. These two terms are sometimes used interchangeably, but there are usually some basic differences.

Both deal with electric current, and of course there could be no electronic devices without the power provided by electricity. But from a technical and career viewpoint, the two fields deal with the use of electric current in different ways.

Electricians and related workers generally handle equipment that is based on the flow of current, while persons working in electronics concentrate on devices based on short pulses of electricity. An electron device changes the current's direction or frequency to make it function as a signal that represents sounds, images, numbers, or other information. This basic difference separates many kinds of electrical and electronic items.

Electricians, for example, tend to work with electric motors, transformers, electric lighting, and so forth. A typical job performed by an electrician might be installing the wiring in a new house or office building or rewiring a large motor used in an industrial setting.

Technicians and others involved in electronics tend to deal with devices such as microprocessors and other equipment using integrated circuits. For example, a career in electronics may involve working with computers, tape recorders, or broadcasting equipment.

A basic understanding of electricity is needed by anyone who works in electronics, and the distinction between the two concepts is not uniformly observed. But in choosing educational programs, applying for jobs, or other activities, it is important to be aware of the general boundaries of each field.

DEVELOPMENT OF ELECTRONICS

The development of electronics is a recent part of human history. Although the existence of electricity has been recognized (if not fully understood) for hundreds of years, the rise of electronics has occurred only in about the last century.

The invention of gas-discharge tubes in the late 1800s, and the later development of vacuum tubes, contributed to the growth of electronics. The first widespread application of tubes began in the 1920s in radio, which helped usher in the modern world. Vacuum tubes were also instrumental in the development of television and early computers.

In the late 1940s and early 1950s, the development of solid-state technology greatly accelerated the growth of electronics. Solid-state devices, in which a signal passes through a solid material instead of through a vacuum, represented a great improvement over technology based on vacuum tubes. Even more revolutionary was the invention in the early 1960s of integrated circuits, in which tiny chips of silicon or some other semiconductor material could do the same work as a bulky transistor. This technology led to the development of microprocessors and the advanced electronic devices we enjoy today.

Over the last three decades, the growth of electronics technology has expanded tremendously, and more and more sophisticated electronic items have begun to play a part in everyday life.

Some of the most important influences on the development of electronics technologies have included the following:

- the development of radio, television, facsimile (fax) machines, and other means of communicating over distances

- advances in transportation, including air and space travel
- the invention and growing use of computers in virtually all aspects of life
- developments in warfare and military technology, with various sophisticated weapons and weapons systems demanding new and improved uses of electronics
- the growing uses of electronic devices in home entertainment
- the invention of robots and automated manufacturing processes
- changes in design and production of electronic devices, which have made them more affordable and thus more widely available

ADVANTAGES OF AN ELECTRONICS CAREER

A career in electronics offers a number of potential benefits. These advantages include the following.

1. *Good salaries and wages.* Most people who work in the field of electronics earn salaries or wages that compare quite favorably with other fields. In fact, some jobs in this area bring salaries that are significantly higher than the average for all occupations. Because many of these jobs require special knowledge and skills, employers often will pay excellent salaries or wages to attract employees who possess the necessary background. In some cases, electronics personnel

can earn several times the average compensation paid to unskilled workers.

Also, men and women employed in electronics may receive a variety of attractive fringe benefits. Such benefits may include medical insurance, retirement plans, vacation pay, support to pursue additional education, profit sharing, or other benefits. Earnings and benefits are discussed further in Chapter 8.

2. *Long-range job potential.* It may sound trite to claim that electronics represents the wave of the future, but there is a great deal of truth in such a statement. After all, it would be difficult to pick an area where more potential for the future exists! Recent changes in electronics have been so immense that people often compare today's reality to the vision of some science fiction writer of decades past, and experts predict even more changes in the future. People in all walks of life depend heavily on the work performed by specialists in electronics, and this trend is expected not only to continue, but to grow.

In choosing a career, an important factor should be its potential to survive in a rapidly changing world. Unfortunately for the persons holding them, many jobs disappear forever as they are displaced by changing technology and economic conditions.

Although this is a possibility in any field, it seems less likely in electronics than in many other career areas. To the contrary, this is a field that tends to thrive on change. Many jobs in electronics are close to what some experts call the cutting edge of advancing technology. As a result, electronics is less vulnerable to change than many other career areas.

3. *Challenging work assignments.* Would you rather design microchips in an electronics lab or bag potato chips in a grocery store? Of course there is a great deal of room between one extreme and the other, and there is nothing wrong with working in a store or performing other respectable work that may require little or no special knowledge or training. However, many workers in unskilled jobs find their work boring and without a sense of challenge, as well as less rewarding in terms of income, benefits, and future potential.

Persons employed in electronics, on the other hand, often find the work itself truly interesting. Designing an electronic device or diagnosing and repairing an equipment problem can provide variety, mental stimulation, and a high degree of job satisfaction.

4. *A comfortable work environment.* Most work performed by people employed in electronics takes place indoors. This might consist of any of a number of settings including a workroom in a small business, a shop or laboratory in an engineering firm, or various locations within a large manufacturing plant. In some cases, the workplace will be the same each day, while in others, job assignments will involve moving from one location to another. For example, a technician might travel to different businesses or visit

people's homes to service or repair electronic equipment. Such an arrangement can be particularly interesting for men and women who enjoy change and variety in their daily routine.

In any instance, working in electronics usually offers the advantage of comfortable environments and relatively low levels of physical exertion compared to highly physical jobs such as construction work, farming, or heavy industrial production.

5. *Mobility.* Once you obtain skills in electronics, they can serve you virtually anywhere in the civilized world, as well as in your home community. This means that you need not move far away to find a good job, unless you live in a remote rural area where technical jobs opportunities are limited. If you prefer to explore new locations, the chances are excellent of landing a job that will take you to a new city, state, or province of your choice.

After all, most electronic fields represent areas where skilled workers are in high demand. So if you acquire the necessary training and skills, you should be able to find a job nearly anywhere.

6. *A wide range of educational choices.* Although some type of training probably will be needed, you can choose from a variety of educational options. A bachelor's degree may be needed to pursue a career in electronic engineering, but many technician's jobs require far less training. In fact,

many educational programs take two years or fewer to complete.

In addition, you can choose formal training in a school or college or another approach such as an apprenticeship or on-the-job training program. The end result is that you can select the type of educational program that best suits your own abilities and preferences. Educational choices are detailed in Chapter 7.

REVIEWING OPTIONS

The options for a career in electronics are many. To learn more, consult the following chapters.

Chapter 2 provides an overview of the types of careers available, along with a look at future prospects. Chapter 3 covers repair of home entertainment equipment, while repair of industrial electronics equipment is discussed in Chapter 4.

Chapter 5 looks at electronics engineering and engineering technology. Several other related career areas are discussed in Chapter 6. Training programs are discussed in Chapter 7, and earnings and benefits are covered in Chapter 8.

Chapter 9 examines special certifications and electronics organizations, and Chapter 10 concludes with observations on the wide range of opportunities offered by a career in electronics and advice on landing a job in the field.

Several appendices are also provided, including information on schools and colleges providing appropriate training programs.

CHAPTER 2

ELECTRONICS IN THE 21ST CENTURY

If you work in electronics, you'll be connected to some of the most rapidly changing areas of modern technology. The entire computer arena, for example, is linked to the advances of electronics. The same is true of various industries ranging from communications to transportation. With the vital role that electronics plays in so many areas, the future of the field holds great promise.

CAREER OPTIONS IN ELECTRONICS

Men and women who work in electronics hold a wide range of jobs. These include the following major categories of employment:

- repairing electronic equipment used primarily in home entertainment
- repairing and maintaining electronic equipment for commercial and industrial use

- designing, testing, and supervising the manufacture of electronic equipment
- operating, servicing, or repairing equipment in specialized areas such as broadcasting

A brief description of each area follows, and more details about these occupations are provided in later chapters.

REPAIR OF HOME ENTERTAINMENT EQUIPMENT

With the proliferation of electronic devices and systems used for personal entertainment or home convenience, an entire support industry of servicing and repairing such equipment has arisen and expanded.

Among the first workers of this type were radio repair persons, and after that, those who provided the same type of services for television sets. Today, technicians known as electronic home equipment repairers (or simply as service technicians or electronic technicians) work with a variety of electronic devices found in the home—for example, videocassette recorders, stereo systems, microwave ovens, and home security systems.

These technicians service working equipment and repair malfunctioning items. Some specialize in a single type of equipment, such as videocassette players and recorders, while others work with a variety of equipment types. Their jobs involve not just the technical tasks involved, but also the human relations element of dealing directly with customers and, in some cases, going into private residences to provide on-site service.

Technicians in this area may be self-employed operators of their own small businesses, or they may work for various types of employers, including small or medium-sized companies specializing in equipment and repair services or large retail firms that sell electronic equipment and then provide the support services needed to keep it in good working order.

REPAIR OF COMMERCIAL AND INDUSTRIAL ELECTRONIC EQUIPMENT

Technicians who install and repair electronic equipment for businesses and other organizations fall under the general category of commercial and industrial electronics technicians. They also may be identified as industrial electronics technicians or other similar job titles.

Men and women employed in this area work with equipment such as antennas, automated manufacturing equipment controls, radar systems, guidance controls for rockets and missiles, industrial robots, and diagnostic equipment used in hospitals and other medical facilities.

They are employed throughout the United States and Canada in a variety of industries. This includes working for large corporations, smaller companies, and other organizations ranging from health care agencies and educational institutions to government agencies and the military.

ELECTRONICS ENGINEERING AND ENGINEERING TECHNOLOGY

At the opposite end of the spectrum from equipment repair is the design and manufacture of electronic systems, devices, and components. These functions are performed by engineers and engineering technologists or technicians.

Engineers, who require the highest level of education of the careers discussed here (usually at least a bachelor's degree), develop, test, and oversee the production or installation of electronic devices or systems. They may specialize in different areas such as radar systems, computer design, electronic controls used in automated manufacturing, or development of sound equipment.

Engineering technologists and technicians perform similar work, but usually under the supervision of engineers. While engineers may be heavily involved in the theory behind a given engineering problem, the technologist or technician generally provides a more hands-on role. For example, a person in this area may assemble a piece of equipment that has been designed by an engineer, and then the two may work together to test and improve it.

Positions in both areas can be found across the United States and Canada in a wide range of industries as well as in the military services.

SPECIALIZED ELECTRONICS AREAS

A number of careers provide opportunities to specialize in one type of electronic equipment or within a single industry.

Broadcasting

For example, broadcast technicians work in the radio and television industries. They operate and maintain the equipment used for recording and transmitting information.

Computer Service and Repair

Another specialty area is computer service and repair. With computers playing an increasingly central role throughout most segments of society, a growing demand exists for persons who can maintain and repair them.

Computer service technicians provide this function for companies that sell computer equipment as well as for organizations large enough to hire their own staff for this purpose. These technicians service and repair not only the computers themselves, but also such related equipment as various types of printers. They also install computer systems and test them for defects.

Other Areas

Workers in several other areas also provide specialized services that include applications in electronics. Positions as communications equipment mechanics, elevator installers and repairers, home appliance and power tool repairers, office machine and cash register servicers, telephone installers, and vending machine servicers and repairers are but a few.

JOB TITLES

Among the job titles listed in the *Dictionary of Occupational Titles* in electronics are:

electromechanical assembler
electromechanical technician
electromedical-equipment repairer
electronic-communications technician
electronic-component processor
electronic-production-line maintenance mechanic
electronic sales-and-service technician
electronics assembler
electronics assembler, prototype
electronics-design engineer

electronics inspector
electronics mechanic
electronics-research engineer
electronics technician
electronics-test engineer
electronics tester
electronics utility worker
electronic technician, nuclear reactor

BACKGROUND AND SKILLS NEEDED

Electronics careers may hold significant promise, but it is important to keep individual abilities and interests in mind when considering the various options available. Just as in other occupations, not everyone is well-suited to an electronics career.

In considering the possibilities, take into account the following factors. Most people should possess (or be able to develop) most or all of the following traits to work effectively in electronics and to enjoy the experience.

1. The *ability to work with hand tools.* This might vary from screwdrivers or soldering guns to voltage meters, but the ability to use tools and items such as meters and scopes—or to learn to use them—is a must for all but the most theoretical work in electronics.

2. *Good math skills.* This is more important in engineering than in many service jobs, but any study of the theory behind electronics requires that information be expressed and understood in mathematical terms. Persons who enjoy math and are good at it have a real edge in this field. For those who feel they lack math abilities, it may be possible to improve the situation through remedial courses or other efforts.

3. *An aptitude for solving problems.* Much work in electronics revolves around the solving of problems. A new design for an electronic component that does not work as planned, or a malfunctioning control system in a manufacturing plant's assembly line, for example, presents problems that must be solved. If you like to work jigsaw or crossword puzzles, figure out ways of fixing cars or household appliances, or even outwit video games, these may be signs of such an aptitude. Special tests available from counselors also can help determine aptitudes in this direction.

4. *A willingness to learn.* Electronics is a complicated subject. To succeed in this area, you must be willing to learn fundamentals as well as a variety of practical applications. This usually means reading and studying textbooks and manuals as well as putting in practice time in a shop or laboratory setting. Such efforts may take place within any number of settings, ranging from vocational schools or colleges to on-the-job training programs. Whatever the type of

instruction involved, the time and energy needed to master it must be something you are willing to commit.

5. *Patience and attention to detail.* The work involved in electronics seldom can be hurried. Instead, it requires patient adherence to details that might seem trivial to the uninformed observer. But considering the delicate and precise nature of much electronic equipment, and the safety factors involved in devices that utilize electricity, patience and attention to detail are absolutely necessary.

Certainly, your basic abilities and aptitudes are only part of the equation for a successful career in electronics. Many other factors also are involved, and these details are reviewed in subsequent chapters. But if, after assessing your own potential, you feel optimistic about an electronics career, the opportunity to follow up on this ambition awaits you.

FUTURE PROSPECTS

A career in electronics can offer a bright future. Studies conducted by the U.S. Department of Labor have found that in most career areas related to electronics, growth in new jobs is expected to occur at a faster rate than that for the average of all career areas.

Not only will jobs be available for those who are qualified, but this field represents one of the most promising areas for the future in terms of new and interesting developments. Enormous changes have occurred in recent years in the way electronic devices affect everyone's life. Even more can be expected in the future. For those who pursue careers in electronics, the potential exists to be at the cutting edge of technological development.

CHAPTER 3

ELECTRONIC HOME ENTERTAINMENT EQUIPMENT REPAIR

What home in North America has no electronic equipment? In most families, a normal part of everyday life is entertainment provided through electronic means. The result is that persons who enjoy hands-on work with electronics can pursue a challenging career in servicing and repairing equipment used in the home. This career area has broadened in recent years in response to the growing popularity of various types of home entertainment based on electronic equipment.

An American or Canadian family may own any number of electronic devices used primarily for entertainment purposes. The great majority of homes have at least one television set, for example, and many have two or more. Videocassette players, also called videocassette recorders (VCRs), have become commonplace. In homes with children, electronic video games are hardly more unusual than baseballs or dolls. Radios, audio cassette players, compact disc players, and other types of musical equipment enrich the lives of people of all ages.

With these and other items becoming an increasingly integral part of everyday home life, the need to service and repair electronic equipment of this type is an expanding one. After all, even the best equipment is not indestructible. Parts become dirty or wear out, units become damaged though household accidents or improper care, and routine maintenance must be performed. Yet because of the complex nature of most electronic components, only a specially trained technician can perform the required work. When this need is combined with the large volume of electronic equipment used for home entertainment, the result is a career area with significant potential.

WORK PERFORMED

Men and women who work as electronic home equipment repairers also may be known as service technicians or electronic technicians. They service equipment that is still functioning properly, diagnose problems, and make repairs. Some technicians work with a variety of equipment types, while others specialize in just one item, such as television sets. Work performed on other electronic items not actually used for entertainment also may fit into this area. For example, service technicians may work with microwave ovens, various kitchen appliances, burglar alarms, and multifaceted home security systems.

In carrying out their work, these technicians may perform tasks such as:

- reading service manuals or wiring diagrams
- running a multipart check of the various components of an electronic device or system
- identifying defective parts
- replacing worn or broken parts
- operating testing equipment such as oscilloscopes or voltage meters
- making adjustments in electronic controls
- cutting or connecting wires
- joining metal components together with a soldering gun
- removing or installing solid-state electronic components
- operating a variety of tools and equipment ranging from pliers and screwdrivers to signal generators and frequency counters
- lifting or transporting equipment
- driving a car, truck, or van to make service calls
- talking with customers to determine problems or explain repairs
- writing reports about servicing or repairs
- calculating bills for parts and service

Men and women who work in this field must be able to concentrate on the task at hand and to work methodically and carefully. They must evaluate problems with equipment and then determine the appropriate course of action. In many instances, they also need to communicate effectively with customers.

In many ways, the work performed by service technicians is similar to that of technicians employed in industry. Persons who have been trained for work in industry, or who have been employed in the commercial sector, may find it relatively easy to branch off into this career area if they so choose. The same is true of those who have been trained in electronics in the military

PLACES OF EMPLOYMENT

Men and women who repair home electronic equipment are employed throughout North America. Many jobs can be found in metropolitan areas, where the population is large. Others can be found in smaller cities and towns where retail stores selling electronic equipment are located, or where there is sufficient population to support a service or repair business. Employers in this field include:

- large department stores that maintain their own service departments
- stores specializing in musical equipment, home appliances, or a range of electronic equipment
- businesses that do not sell equipment but specialize in repairs and service
- self-operated businesses

The latter represents a promising alternative for those persons who prefer to operate their own businesses rather than work for another employer. Some service technicians work out of their homes, where they maintain a shop located in a basement, garage, or workroom dedicated to this purpose. Others operate out of a shop or store they build, buy, or lease. They may serve as the only technician or may hire others who work under their supervision. In this case, their duties may include supervising employees, completing business reports, and other managerial functions.

WORKING ENVIRONMENT

Service technicians and related workers usually perform their jobs in comfortable working environments. This might consist of a shop setting to which customers bring their equipment for repairs and service, or, in some cases, it might mean going into people's homes to provide on-site work. In either case, technicians in this field avoid the discomfort faced by some workers of having a job outdoors or in a noisy, assembly-line setting.

A typical shop setting will include good lighting, air conditioning or heating, and workbenches or counters designed for easy access. In some cases, the environment is quite informal, and technicians may be allowed to listen to radios or tape players while working. Informal, comfortable clothes are also the norm, although some companies may ask workers to wear smocks or some type of standardized clothing. For self-employed technicians, all of these factors are determined according to the worker's own preferences.

For technicians who go to customers' homes to make service calls, working environments will vary. Some people enjoy this kind of variety in work settings. One job might take them to an apartment building, another to a huge mansion, and another to a house in the suburbs. At the same time, they come in contact with many different people of all ages and backgrounds. For people who become bored easily working in the same setting, this can be a real plus. Even the time spent driving to and from job sites can provide a change of pace. Of course, for those who prefer a highly structured setting, these same factors can become liabilities rather than assets.

Technicians sometimes may need to move or carry heavy items, such as television sets or microwave ovens, so they must guard against injuries caused from lifting or dropping equipment or from falling while moving larger items. They also need to observe careful safety procedures to avoid electrical shock or burns. In general, however, this is not a particularly hazardous career area.

THE RIGHT SKILLS AND APTITUDES

Persons who hope to work in home entertainment equipment repair should have the same basic aptitudes as those who plan to work in industry. These include:
- problem-solving abilities
- the ability to work with hand tools, electronic measurement devices, and other tools and equipment

- sufficient math skills to complete required courses and understand basic electronic theory
- patience
- good working habits

In addition, it helps to have good human relations skills. Quite often, technicians must discuss equipment problems with owners, explain the nature of repairs, estimate costs, and interact in other ways. Those who get along well with other people and communicate effectively may have a special advantage in working in this field.

GETTING TRAINED

To prepare for a career in this field, some type of training will be necessary. Such instruction might come in the form of on-the-job training or an apprenticeship. For example, the service division of a large retail firm may hire a person who has had little or no special training in electronics, and then provide short-term classes or assign the individual to assist experienced workers and learn repair techniques in the process. This can be a relatively informal training program or a more formal apprenticeship, although the latter is not as common in this specialty area as in the commercial and industrial area.

Many persons prepare for this field by attending a vocational school, trade school, or two-year college. Some programs, especially those in noncollegiate vocational schools, concentrate in a single area such as television repair. Others provide several options from which students can select.

For example, students who attend Ohio's Edison State Community College can acquire these in skills in three different ways:

1. By taking electronics courses of their choice to gain specialized knowledge but without pursuing a formal program of study;
2. By pursuing a certificate program that consists almost entirely of electronics and related courses and can be completed in a year of full-time study;
3. By completing an associate degree (two-year) program that includes not only electronics courses, but also other subjects designed to enhance their background. Students can select from a Digital Systems Technology or Industrial Electronics Technology degree program.

Many courses in the associate degree programs are transferrable to four-year colleges and universities, although their primary purpose is job preparation rather than transferability. Students completing this program have gone on to attend Bowling Green State University, the University of Dayton, the University of Toledo, and a number of others. While persons planning to work as service technicians may not pursue additional education, the fact that courses may be transferred is valuable if future plans change.

At Edison, as at many other two-year colleges, the programs are designed to meet a wide range of employment objectives in the electrical/electronics field. Many such programs are categorized in areas such as electronics, electrical/electronics technology, or electronics technology, rather than by specific job area. This means that you may not find a program offered specifically for those who plan to work as service technicians, but you instead will take the knowledge learned in a broad-based electronics program and apply it to your field. It also means you will be studying with people who plan to work in industry and in various specialized areas of electronics and, in some cases, with workers who are already employed but updating or expanding their skills. The result can be a positive environment to share information and learn as much as possible about the subjects being covered, especially in a lab setting where you may work in tandem with other students.

For those who want to earn an associate degree, two typical sequences of studies are as follows:

Associate of Applied Science (AAS) in Digital Systems Technology

First Semester
Basic DC Circuits
Advanced DC Circuits
Electronic Devices
Composition I
Technical Writing
Introduction to Spreadsheets
Algebra 4

Second Semester
AC Circuits
Electronic Circuits
Digital Electronics
Electronic Assembly
Printed Circuit Board Layout
College Algebra

Third Semester
Linear Integrated Circuits
Microprocessor Systems I
Microprocessor Systems II
Fundamentals of Economics

C Language
Fundamentals of
    Communication

Fourth Semester
Embedded Controllers
RISC & Fuzzy Logic Topics

Programmable Controllers I
Data Acquisition & Signal
    Processing
Microcomputer Hardware
Introduction to Ethics

Associate of Applied Science (AAS) in Industrial Electronics Technology

First Semester
Basic DC Circuits
Advanced DC Circuits
Electronic Devices
Composition I
Technical Writing
Introduction to Spreadsheets
Algebra 4

Second Semester
AC Circuits
Electronic Circuits
Digital Electronics
Electronic Assembly
Printed Circuit Board Layout
College Algebra

Third Semester
Linear Integrated Circuits

Microprocessor Systems I
Electrical Machinery &
    Control
Microprocessor Systems II
C Language
Fundamentals of
    Communication

Fourth Semester
Industrial Control
    Electronics I
Industrial Control
    Electronics II
Programmable Controllers I
Programmable Controllers II
Fundamentals of Economics
Introduction to Ethics

For most jobs in repairing home equipment, the background provided through a one-year certificate program will provide all the basic skills necessary to find a job and to perform well on the job. The extra courses covered under an associate degree program, although not usually required for service technicians, could nevertheless prove helpful from both an educational standpoint and for potential use in the future. In either case, a completed degree or certificate should give you a competitive edge over persons who have not had such training.

Several of these electronics courses would have special appeal to those interested in careers as service technicians, including the following.

In the Electronic Devices course (which carries 3 semester credits), students learn about semiconductor diodes, transistors, and field effect transistors (FETs). The course also covers bias stability requirements and analysis of bias circuitry; operational characteristics of FET and diode switching circuits; and component testing and evaluation.

In Digital Electronics (offered for 4 credits), students learn the fundamentals of digital electronics. The course includes number systems and codes peculiar to digital systems, design and analysis of combinational logic circuitry, and other basics of digital electronics.

Other courses cover various aspects of electronics, many of which can be applied to the home equipment repair field.

Programs and courses of this type vary from one school to another, but they are widely available. More details on selecting a school or college are provided in Chapter 7.

CHAPTER 4

COMMERCIAL AND INDUSTRIAL ELECTRONICS EQUIPMENT REPAIR

Want to see a high-demand area for electronics technicians? Try the installation and repair of equipment for businesses, the military, or other organizations. People who perform this function may be designated as commercial and industrial electronics technicians, or more simply as industrial electronics technicians.

JOB DUTIES

Working in this area may involve completing tasks such as these:

- installing electronic components of a radar system at a commercial airport
- setting up special electronic equipment used to diagnose illnesses in hospitals
- repairing components of an automated assembly line in a manufacturing plant

- cleaning and servicing an industrial robot
- repairing a malfunctioning component of a missile tracking system at a military base
- installing a radio transmitter for a new radio station

Completion of these and other related tasks may require the ability to:

- use electronic tools such as ohmmeters, voltage meters, oscilloscopes, and signal generators
- use simple hand tools such as pliers, wire cutters, or screwdrivers
- read blueprints, wiring diagrams, or equipment specifications
- maintain logs of service and repairs for a specific system or piece of equipment
- test and calibrate electronic components
- identify reasons equipment has malfunctioned
- replace defective electronic components
- install or replace wiring for an electronic system
- clean dirty parts of a piece of equipment or an entire system

Technicians working in this field may perform a wide range of jobs. The *Dictionary of Occupational Titles* lists the following responsibilities, which may be covered by this and related positions:

Repairs electronic equipment, such as computers, industrial controls, radar systems, telemetering and missile control systems, transmitters, antennas, and servomechanisms, following blueprints and manufacturers' specifications, and using handtools and test instruments: tests faulty equipment and applies knowledge of functional operation of electronic units and systems to diagnose cause of malfunction. Tests electronic components and circuits to locate defects, using oscilloscopes, signal generators, ammeters, and voltmeters. Replaces defective components and wiring and adjusts mechanical parts, using handtools and soldering iron. Aligns, adjusts, and calibrates equipment according to specifications. Calibrates testing instruments. Maintains records of repairs, calibrations, and tests. May install equipment in industrial or military establishments and in aircraft and missiles. May operate equipment, such as communication equipment and missile control systems, in ground and flight tests, and be required to hold license from governmental agency.

WORKING CONDITIONS

Electronics technicians work in a variety of settings. A typical job site might be a room or shop area devoted to repair and servicing of equipment. Such an environment usually will feature good lighting, controlled levels of temperature and humidity, and an overall work setting that is consistently comfortable. The work environment is generally somewhat casual, where employees wear informal clothes and feel free to talk among themselves or play soft music while working.

Not all jobs or tasks are performed in such a setting, however. Technicians may repair or service equipment where it is used rather than in a central servicing facility. This situation can take workers to a wide range of settings, such as assembly lines, different offices within a large organization, manufacturing facilities, construction sites, military bases, or other locations where electronic equipment is used. Inevitably, some sites will be less pleasant than others, but an offsetting factor is the variety workers may enjoy in the process.

In general, electronics technicians can count on favorable working conditions. Because electronic devices may be sensitive to humidity, temperature extremes, and other environmental features, they usually are located in areas that also are comfortable to human beings. The end result is that technicians usually avoid the discomfort sometimes experienced by those who must work outdoors or in other physically challenging settings.

BACKGROUND AND TRAINING NEEDED

Persons who hope to work as electronic technicians in the industrial or commercial sector should demonstrate most or all of the aptitudes discussed in Chapter 2. Of particular importance is an orientation to addressing and solving problems.

In addition, some type of training generally will be necessary to work in this field. This might consist of vocational classes offered at the high school level or through an adult education program, training in a technical or proprietary school, an apprenticeship, or on-the-job training (Chapter 7 offers further discussion of these options).

A frequent path to a career in this area is completion of an electronics program offered by a two-year college. Such programs are offered in many community, junior, and technical colleges.

For example, Delaware County Community College in Media, Pennsylvania, offers an associate degree program in electronics technology. The program, which can be completed in two years of full-time study, prepares students to perform such tasks as the following:

- identifying malfunctions in electrical and electromechanical instruments
- repairing instruments that are not functioning properly
- calibrating instruments used for industrial or scientific purposes
- providing equipment maintenance using standard procedures
- testing input-output parameters of electronic devices
- assembling scientific and industrial test equipment

- identifying electronic devices or systems
- presenting technical information in oral and written formats

A typical course of study under this program would extend over four academic semesters as follows, although students can take longer than two years if they desire to attend part-time or simply take fewer courses at any one time:

First Semester
English Composition I
Technical Mathematics I
Technical Physics I
DC Circuits
Basic Technical Skills

Second Semester
English Composition II
Technical Mathematics II
Program Design and Development
Electronics I

Third Semester
AC Analysis
Electronics II
Electro-Mechanical Technology
Humanities Elective
Social Science Elective

Fourth Semester
Microprocessors I
Career Elective
Linear Integrated Circuits
Internship or Electronics Elective

The content of electronics courses such as these provides students with detailed background in the key areas needed to work in industry following program completion.

For example, students enrolling in Electronics I learn to perform tasks such as the following:

- analyze the behavior of simple diode circuits
- analyze the behavior of single-stage transistor amplifier circuits and of single-stage field-effect amplifier circuits
- follow schematic diagrams to connect simple circuits
- build DC rectifier circuits and measure their ripple factor
- build single-stage transistor amplifier circuits and measure their gain
- test diodes, transistors, and field-effect transistors for proper operation.

In the Digital Electronics course, students learn about digital techniques and circuits, including the operation of digital logic gates as well as integrated circuit families used in digital equipment. By the end of the course, successful students are able to:

- discuss the applications and advantages in using digital techniques
- implement logic functions using standard digital logic gates
- discuss the operation of flip-flops, counters, and shift registers
- design elementary digital circuits

At Haywood Community College in Clyde, North Carolina, all students in Electronic Engineering Technology take the following courses

First-Year Courses
Technical Drafting
Intro to Computers
Intro to Technology
CADD for Electronics
C++ Programming
DC/AC Circuit Analysis
Algebra/Trig II

Second-Year Courses
Electronic Devices
Digital Electronics
Physics-Mechanics
Industrial Controls
Linear IC Applications
Intro to Microprocessors
Lasers and Applications
Intro to PLCs

In addition, students take seven technical courses in areas such as robotics and drafting, plus several general education courses such as expository writing and psychology.

Not all two-year colleges offer programs in electronics, but most technical colleges and many community colleges include such programs among their standard offerings. Many also feature their own variations of electronics programs. For instance, Indiana Vocational Technical College students may specialize in industrial electronics or in communication technology. Other colleges may offer options in automation instrumentation, fiber optics communications, or other areas. To determine what is available at any college, consult its catalog or contact the admissions office or the electronics department.

QUESTIONS TO ASK YOURSELF

If you think a career in this area sounds appealing, consider the following basic questions:

1. Do you enjoy working with your hands?
2. Are you good with tools?
3. Are you curious about technical matters (for example, wondering how a certain device works)?
4. If you become a student, will you be able to handle the math involved?

5. Can you picture yourself working in an industrial or commercial environment, spending most of your time working on electronic equipment?
6. Are you patient?
7. Do you have good eyesight (or can vision problems be corrected with glasses or contact lenses)?
8. Can you effectively read (or learn to read) technical material such as blueprints, diagrams, and manuals?
9. Have you finished high school, or are you on track to high school completion?
10. Are you willing to complete additional education?

If you can answer "yes" to most or all of these questions, then a career in commercial or industrial equipment repair may be well worth pursuing.

CHAPTER 5

ELECTRONICS ENGINEERING AND ENGINEERING TECHNOLOGY

Some of the most interesting careers in electronics can be found in the areas of engineering and engineering technology. Electronics engineers and technologists perform a wide range of important functions.

ENGINEERING VERSUS ENGINEERING TECHNOLOGY

Although terminology can be confusing, some basic differences exist between these two areas, both of which also differ from other electronics occupations discussed in previous chapters.

Electronic engineering technologists (also sometimes called technicians, although their work may be on a different level than service technicians or related workers) perform work that in some ways is similar to that done by

43

engineers but differs in that it usually involves applications more than theory. In other words, it has more of a hands-on focus. For instance, an engineer may design a new component or piece of equipment used on an automated assembly line. The new design is turned over to an engineering technologist, who installs the new component and tests its capabilities.

Generally, less education is required to become an engineering technologist, although this is not always the case. Many community and technical colleges offer associate degrees in electronic engineering technology or related areas, which can be completed in two years of full-time study. Most engineering degrees, on the other hand, take at least four years as a full-time student to complete. More information on these programs and other educational options is covered in Chapter 7.

Because more education is needed and responsibilities may be greater, the following statements often are true for electronics engineering when compared to engineering technology:

- Electronics engineering may be a more difficult field to enter, with many colleges requiring that students have excellent high school grades and high scores on standardized tests (such as the ACT or SAT exam) just to get admitted to an engineering program.
- Some engineering courses are more difficult than corresponding courses in engineering technology. A deeper understanding of math and physics may be necessary.

- Not only is the minimum educational level for electronics engineers a bachelor's degree, but many engineers hold master's degrees or other advanced degrees.
- Engineers tend to earn the highest salaries of any electronics occupations.
- Engineers are more likely to move into management positions than those holding other types of electronics positions.

DUTIES OF ENGINEERING TECHNOLOGISTS

Persons functioning as engineering technologists or technicians often work under the supervision of engineers, or they may work in close coordination with other types of personnel.

The *Dictionary of Occupational Titles* provides the following job description for an electronics technician in the engineering area:

> Applies electronic theory, principles of electrical circuits, electrical testing procedures, engineering mathematics, physics, and related knowledge to lay out, build, test, troubleshoot, repair, and modify developmental and production electronic equipment, such as computers, missile-control instrumentation, and machine tool numerical controls: Discusses layout and assembly problems with electronics engineer and draws sketches to clarify design details and

functional criteria of electronic units. Assembles experimental circuitry or complete prototype model according to engineering instructions, technical manuals, and knowledge of electronic systems and components and their functions. Recommends changes in circuitry or installation specifications to simplify assembly and maintenance. Sets up standard test apparatus or contrives test equipment and circuitry, and conducts functional, operational, environmental, and life tests to evaluate performance and reliability of prototype or production model. Analyzes and interprets test data. Adjusts, calibrates, aligns, and modifies circuitry and components and records effects on unit performance. Writes technical reports and develops charts, graphs, and schematics to describe and illustrate systems operating characteristics, malfunctions, deviations from design specifications, and functional limitations for consideration by professional engineering personnel in broader determinations affecting systems design and laboratory procedures. May operate bench lathes, drills and other machine tools to fabricate nonprocurable items, such as coils, terminal boards, and chassis. May check out newly installed equipment in airplanes, ships, and structures to evaluate system performance under actual operating conditions. May instruct and supervise lower grade technical personnel. May be designated according to specialization in electronic applications.

Typical jobs undertaken by an electronics engineering technician may include:

- assisting an engineer in designing a prototype for a new kind of medical testing equipment
- writing specifications for a key component of a radar system
- assembling a controlling device for an automated manufacturing system
- diagnosing a problem in malfunctioning radio equipment
- adjusting and improving movement of an industrial robot
- writing a computer program as a part of an automated manufacturing production line
- repairing a piece of malfunctioning navigation equipment
- using computer-aided design (CAD) techniques to help develop a temperature-control device in a chemical plant
- preparing a series of experiments using electronic devices in cooperation with a scientist or engineer

DUTIES OF ELECTRONICS ENGINEERS

Engineering differs from engineering technology in that it tends to be based more extensively on theoretical concepts. Engineers must consider why things happen and then use their background to solve problems, design systems, and perform other broad-based functions.

The *Dictionary of Occupational Titles* lists the following duties for an electronics engineer:

> Conducts research and development activities concerned with design, manufacture, and testing of electronic components, products, and systems, and in development of applications of products to commercial, industrial, medical, military, and scientific uses: Designs electrical circuits, electronic components, and integrated systems, using ferroelectric, nonlinear, dielectric, phosphor, photoconductive, and thermoelectric properties of materials. Designs and directs engineering personnel in fabrication of test control apparatus and equipment, and determines procedures for testing products. Develops new applications of electrical and dielectric properties in metallic and nonmetallic materials used in components, and in application of components to products or systems. May develop field operation and maintenance of electronic installations. May evaluate operational systems and recommend design modifications to eliminate causes of malfunctions or changes in system requirements. May specialize in development of electronic principles and technology in fields, such as telecommunications, telemetry, aerospace guidance, missile propulsion control, countermeasures, acoustics, nucleonic instrumentation, industrial controls and measurements, high-frequency heating, laboratory techniques, computers, electronic data processing and

reduction, teaching aids and techniques, radiation detection, encephalography, electron optics, and biomedical research.

Typical tasks undertaken by an electronics engineer might include:

- designing new electronic devices such as computers or medical monitoring equipment
- adapting or improving components of an existing device (for example, an airplane's autopilot unit)
- working as a member of a team to design a complex system such as a robot control system
- writing computer software needed for use of electronic equipment
- testing equipment (for example, an automated device used to control an assembly line) to assess capabilities or deficiencies
- establishing performance standards for electronic equipment
- developing maintenance schedules for electronic devices and systems
- analyzing and solving problems in equipment operation
- estimating the cost of work to be performed
- supervising technicians and other technical personnel
- seeing that safety standards are met in use or production of electronic equipment
- completing research or production reports

PLACES OF EMPLOYMENT

Electronics engineers and engineering technologists enjoy a great deal of diversity in the types of jobs available. They are employed by a wide range of companies and organizations. Examples include engineering consulting firms, computer manufacturers, research and development firms, utility companies, manufacturers of electronic equipment, and many others. In addition, some work for government agencies ranging from the National Aeronautics and Space Administration (NASA) to the U.S. Department of Energy, as well as in the military.

The biggest proportion of jobs can be found in large and medium-sized cities, but jobs can be found across the United States and Canada as well as in other countries around the world.

WORKING ENVIRONMENT

Like others following electronics careers, persons employed as engineers and engineering technologists often work in comfortable surroundings. Some engineers have their own private offices, and even those who work in a shared work space may have certain amenities such as their own personal computer and access to secretarial help.

In some cases, significant travel may be involved. An engineer employed for a large corporation, for example, may travel to plants or work sites around the country or even internationally. This can be an interesting experience for those who enjoy seeing new places.

EDUCATIONAL PREPARATION

Completion of a college-level program is a must to prepare for employment in this area. The level of studies varies.

For those in electronics engineering technology, subjects studied are somewhat similar to those noted in previous chapters, but with more math and physics as a basic requirement. At Mesa Community College in Mesa, Arizona, for example, students must meet an algebra requirement before beginning the electronic engineering technology program. For this purpose, most enroll in a special course called Beginning Algebra for Technology. They then complete the following required courses:

Engineering Analysis Tools and Techniques
Engineering Problem Solving and Design
DC Circuit Analysis
AC Circuit Analysis
Solid-State Devices & Circuits
Digital Logic and Circuits

Computer Programming for Technology
Linear Solid-State Devices
Microprocessor Concepts
Analytic Geometry & Calculus I
Calculus with Analytic Geometry II
General Physics I
General Physics II or Fundamental Chemistry and
    Fundamental Chemistry Laboratory
Freshman English
An oral communication course
A critical reading course
Several other general education courses

These courses provide a broad background in basic electronics concepts as well as the general education required as a portion of a college education. Subjects range from mathematical and scientific theory to hands-on application of engineering technology principles.

For students studying engineering, even more intensive preparation is required. The typical bachelor's level engineering program includes a healthy number of courses in physics (with more emphasis on calculus than in engineering technology programs), math, computer science, specialized engineering courses, and additional general studies requirements. Some programs are so demanding, in fact, that they require five years to complete instead of four.

This is not to indicate that engineering is unreasonably difficult, but anyone planning on such a career should understand that it is considered one of the more challenging areas college students can take. If you are interested, go for it! But be sure to weigh the challenges and advantages of this area against other careers in electronics before going ahead.

CHAPTER 6

SPECIALIZED ELECTRONICS OCCUPATIONS

Some jobs in electronics require similar skills and training as those described in previous chapters, but differ in that they involve work that is specialized to one industry or type of electronic equipment. Following is a brief overview of some of these job categories.

BROADCAST TECHNICIANS

The specialized nature of the radio and television industries requires technicians to operate and maintain the equipment used for recording and transmitting information. Broadcast technicians fill this role by working with equipment such as television cameras, transmitters, microphones, audio-tape recorders, video-tape recorders, and other electronic devices.

Technicians in this field hold a variety of job titles. Examples include:

audio control engineer
recording engineer
video control engineer
field technician
maintenance technician
transmitter operator

In many cases, the term *engineer* is used as a synonym for *technician* and does not necessarily require a college degree in engineering (instead, training at a vocational school or two-year college often will suffice).

Work Performed

Typical jobs performed by broadcast technicians include the following:

- operating equipment in a booth or control room during a television broadcast
- setting up, operating, and dismantling equipment used for a remote-site radio broadcast
- operating transmitters and maintaining broadcast logs
- servicing and repairing electronic broadcasting equipment
- operating sound, lighting, or special effects equipment

Places of Employment

Broadcast technicians work at radio and television stations throughout North America. Most such facilities are located in or near cities, although not all stations are restricted to large metropolitan areas (especially with radio). Some jobs also can be found with universities, corporations, or other organizations that produce training materials, audio tapes, or other broadcast-type materials.

Working Environment

A special advantage experienced by many broadcast technicians is the sense of glamour that often accompanies radio and television work. For example, a technician who assists a television news crew may be exposed to a variety of newsworthy events or encounter famous people. The excitement of working as part of a team striving for high-quality broadcasting also can prove stimulating.

COMPUTER SERVICE TECHNICIANS

Like it or not, the computer is here to stay. Computers are becoming an increasingly vital part of life, not just in high-technology industries, but also in daily life. Almost every company or organization uses computers, accomplishing tasks ranging from word processing and inventory to control of manufacturing processes. This means that demand is growing for persons who can maintain and repair computer equipment.

Computer service technicians hold jobs with firms that sell computers, with companies and large organizations that own large numbers of computers and choose to employ their own service personnel, and with the military. They service and repair computers and related equipment such as printers and disk storage units.

Work Performed

Examples of work performed by computer service technicians include:

- installing computers and computer systems, including hooking up electrical connections and testing equipment before it is used
- running diagnostic programs and identifying equipment malfunctions
- replacing components of computers and related equipment
- cleaning and adjusting equipment such as disk drives, printers, and other components and peripherals
- transporting computer equipment to and from a central repair shop
- calling on customers and maintaining positive relationships with them

Educational Background

The background required for working in this area is much like that needed for other technicians providing service and repair functions. Of course, special emphasis on computers and how they work is a prime component of any preparation for a career in this area.

Working Conditions

One difference between this field and some related areas is that more night or weekend work may be required, at least with some employers. Because computers are so important to the operations of many businesses, malfunctions may require immediate attention. This can mean being on call during night or weekend hours, or, in some cases, putting in shift work.

A plus in such situations may be the opportunity to earn extra income, which is often paid at an overtime rate of one and one-half to two times the normal hourly wage.

Employment Outlook

A strong point for this career area is the growing nature of the field itself. According to U.S. Department of Labor projections, growth of jobs in computer service and repair is expected to be much faster than the average for all occupations in the years ahead. That means more openings will develop for those wanting to break into the field, as well as greater opportunities for those who are employed but who would like to change jobs. The overall outlook is that this is one of today's most promising career areas.

RELATED OCCUPATIONS

Persons who enjoy working with electronic devices may apply such skills in a variety of other job categories. These include the following:

communications equipment mechanics
elevator installers and repairers
home appliance and power tool repairers
office machine and cash register servicers
telephone installers
vending machine servicers and repairers

Job demands, training, and other factors of careers in these fields are similar to those discussed in previous chapters and will not be repeated here. A general background in electronics can provide the basis for branching off into one of these specialty areas.

Another potential job category is that of manager. Technicians or engineers may move into supervisory roles since in many organizations managers are needed to supervise the work of staff.

An interesting program is offered by Southern Illinois University in Carbondale, Illinois. SIU's Bachelor of Science in Electronics Management program is designed for graduates of associate degree programs in electronics who would like to pursue a long-term career in the electronics industry. The program offers students a chance to combine technical and managerial skills.

Students in this program take courses in both electronics and management. The program also includes a general education requirement. Students who have developed specialties in military service (such as radar, ground equipment electronics systems, communications, navigation, and avionic instruments) may build upon their experiences.

Students pursuing this degree option select from the following programs of study:

Biomedical Instrumentation Technology (emphasizing repairing, installing, selling, and managing technology within the medical industry).

Industrial Electronics Technology (repairing, installing, selling, and managing technology associated with robotic and industrial control systems).

Communications Technology (repairing, installing, selling, and managing technology associated with telephone systems, wireless communication, video, and audio equipment).

Microcomputer Technology (repairing or installing microprocessor-based equipment).

In addition to the major areas of employment in electronics, other career areas may include working with electronic devices or principles. For example, automobile technicians working with contemporary cars and trucks may deal with electronic components and testing devices. The same is true for aircraft mechanics (particularly those who specialize in avionics), various types of engineers, physicists, and many others.

The overall outlook is that for persons interested in electronics, plenty of career options are available. The employment possibilities in this area are varied indeed!

CHAPTER 7

OBTAINING THE RIGHT TRAINING

To pursue a career in electronics, you will probably need to complete a special training or educational program. Although some limited possibilities may exist for self-taught workers, most employers expect applicants to have acquired specialized knowledge through a structured training program.

Methods of achieving this knowledge vary. For some jobs at the technician's level, on-the-job training is a possibility. But for the majority of jobs in electronics, the best approach begins with completing an electronics program offered by a school or college. Following such a path involves planning ahead, selecting the right program and institution, and then completing each course required to earn a diploma, certificate, degree, or other credential.

MAKING EDUCATIONAL PLANS

To succeed with any educational effort, it is best to plan ahead in as much detail as possible. Students who make their decisions about education at the last moment often encounter all kinds of difficulties. In fact, educators agree that those who enroll late are much more likely to fail or drop out than are most other students.

In advance planning, consider such facts as the following:

- types of schools offering electronics programs
- location of schools in relation to your home (for example, is a given school within reasonable commuting distance, or will it be necessary to live in a dormitory or apartment?)
- level of educational offerings provided (for example, bachelor's degree, associate degree, or certificate)
- length of time required for program completion
- cost
- availability of financial aid, if needed
- application deadlines
- prerequisites (courses or skills needed before you can be admitted to a given school, its electronics program, or individual courses)
- your own abilities to complete the required work

To plan ahead, you will need to gather information, ask questions, and make decisions. It is important to realize that any efforts you make to complete a training or educational program can pay off for years to come, so be sure to approach this matter with the seriousness it deserves.

REVIEWING EDUCATIONAL OPTIONS

How do you select the right school or college to obtain an appropriate educational background in electronics? A good first step is taking some time to review basic information about the school in general, and specifically about its electronics program (or programs, if more than one is offered).

Don't make the mistake of assuming that all schools or programs are the same, for they may have huge differences. Just because a school is close at hand, for instance, doesn't necessarily mean it is the best choice for you. Or the fact that a representative tries to get you to enroll may not be sufficient reason to choose the program being touted (after all, that is the job of men and women who recruit for colleges and schools). The truth is, schools vary in price, quality, level of instruction, effectiveness in placing graduates in good jobs, and many other factors.

In selecting a school, first make sure it is the right kind of institution for your goals. For example, if you want to work in the repair area, a trade school or vocational school may provide sufficient training. But what if you plan to pursue electronic engineering technology? In most such cases, only a postsecondary institution such as a community or technical college will suffice. For engineering, you will need to attend a four-year school.

Your choices in types of schools may include the following:

1. vocational schools at the secondary (high school) level
2. trade or technical schools

3. two-year colleges
4. four-year colleges and universities

Vocational Schools

If you have not yet finished high school, you may be able to take classes in electronics at your high school or at a nearby school that has been designated as a provider of vocational training for your area. Vocational courses in electronics usually do not offer as much detail at this level as at the postsecondary level, but they can get you started.

If you have already completed school, or if you dropped out without finishing, you may be able to enroll in an adult education program run by a local public school district or vocational school. Such programs often are offered at night to accommodate adults who have other jobs but would like to attain the skills to make a career change. Usually, no special background is needed to qualify for such courses, and they may be offered at low cost or even free of charge.

Trade Schools

Trade schools may be called proprietary schools, technical schools, institutes, or even business, career, or technical colleges, although they are not really colleges in the true sense of the word. Their main purpose is to offer short-term occupational training. Some schools may specialize in just one area. For example, some specialize entirely in electronics training. Others offer a variety of programs in different career fields.

A distinctive feature of trade schools is that they concentrate on the major subject to a greater degree than colleges, and sometimes exclusively. Students who study electronics at a trade school may not be required to take nontechnical courses such as English composition, literature, history, or psychology. This may be seen as an advantage by some students, especially those who have not enjoyed going to school in the past. Not only can other courses be avoided, but the lack of them can speed up the process of completing a training program. In many cases, such a program can be completed in months rather than years.

Of course, life is full of tradeoffs, and this is one area where such differences can be substantial. Be sure to keep in mind the following facts as you consider trade schools versus other types of training opportunities:

1. Courses are not usually transferable. This means that if you decide later to go to college, the classes you completed in trade school will not count for college credits. You will have to start completely over.

2. Trade schools may be expensive. Most of these schools operate as businesses. Unlike other schools that may be subsidized by the government or run on a nonprofit basis, they must make a profit to survive. Thus, fees may be very high compared to public two-year colleges.

An offsetting factor is that financial aid awards may be correspondingly higher, canceling out much of the difference in terms of what you actually pay out of your own pocket. But if part of your financial aid is based on loans, you will be paying back a substantial amount of money over a long period of time. You can be liable for such a loan even if you drop out of school and change your mind about a career in electronics.

3. Reputations vary. Some trade schools have earned excellent reputations among students, companies that employ graduates, and the local communities they serve. But some others are not well regarded, and employers may be less than enthusiastic about hiring their graduates. Because the trade school's ultimate goal is to make a profit, educational quality can sometimes be sacrificed.

This is not to say that you will receive ineffective training at a trade school, but it is best to check out factors related to quality. Some schools advertise that they are registered, certified, or approved by the state or other government agencies, but this often means little more than the payment of a licensing fee and has nothing to do with quality. A better indicator is accreditation by an organization such as the Accrediting Commission of Career Schools and College of Technology. This accreditation should be indicated in school publications; if it is not, chances are the school has not earned such a designation.

Two-Year Colleges

Another option for preparing for a career in electronics is to enroll in a two-year college, which may be called a junior, community, or technical college. Many such colleges offer a choice between (1) a basic program that can be completed in a year or less, or (2) an associate degree program that normally takes two years as a full-time student to complete. The former may be much like programs offered by trade schools, with the advantage that they tend to be much less expensive.

Associate degree programs take longer to finish because students must take classes not just in electronics, but also in other subjects. For example, you might study English composition or technical writing, history, physical education, or sociology. Only a few such classes must be completed, but they are a requirement to earn a two-year college degree.

Another consideration is that many courses completed at two-year colleges can be transferred to four-year colleges and universities. This may or not be in your plans at first, but educational goals often change. Earning credits that can be transferred may be to your advantage in the future. It is important to remember that courses completed at trade schools, by comparison, rarely will be accepted for credit by colleges and universities.

If short-term training leading to a job in electronics is your only goal, you may opt for a program offered by a two-year college that leads to a diploma or certificate instead of a degree. In this case, courses may not be designed for transfer, and you may not need to take courses in general studies. Instead, you will study electronics and closely related subjects exclusively. If such a program is available at a nearby community or technical college, you may find it much more affordable than a trade school.

Four-Year Institutions

Four-year colleges and universities usually do not offer programs to train technicians, although some four-year schools have community college components or other offerings in this area. But for a degree in engineering, a college or university is the only option.

Many large universities and a number of smaller four-year colleges offer programs in electronics engineering or a related area. A few offer four-year programs in engineering technology, although these are not as common.

Many colleges specialize in certain areas (such as the liberal arts) and as a result do not offer engineering programs. To find out if a program is available at any given college or university, consult the college catalog or the admissions office. If you are interested in programs beyond the bachelor's degree, check with the graduate school at any university in which you are potentially interested.

Unlike community colleges, most four-year schools do not practice open admissions. You must meet certain admission requirements, and many schools operate on a competitive basis and accept only a limited number of applicants. Before pursuing a four-year college, be sure to find out how the school admits students, what kind of information is required, and when it must be submitted. Typical requirements include ACT or SAT scores—the higher, the better—and a transcript of your high school courses and grades.

SELECTING A SCHOOL OR COLLEGE

In considering any school or college, take the following steps:

1. *Make sure you know at what level programs are offered.* As previously mentioned, just because a school calls itself a college, that does not necessarily mean it really operates on the collegiate level. To make certain, examine the school's catalog and see whether students earn diplomas, certificates, or associate degrees. Look also at information on transfer programs (if any), relationships with other schools (such as membership in a state community college system), and other basic details.

2. *Consult the catalog for other information.* In reviewing a catalog, take time also to review any sections on electronics programs or courses. Watch for details such as:

- the kinds of jobs graduates are prepared to perform
- how many courses must be completed
- length of time to complete a program

- descriptions of electronics courses
- accreditation (If none is listed, beware. Colleges should be accredited by a regional accrediting group such as the North Central Association of Colleges and Schools, the Southern Association of Colleges and Schools, or the New England Association.)
- admission requirements
- credentials of faculty

3. *Visit the school.* Even if a school you are considering is not a local one, be sure to visit the campus. Enrolling sight unseen can lead to problems. Take a look at electronics labs, classrooms, and other points of interest. Some schools that sound great in their promotional materials are much less attractive in real life, and they may not have the up-to-date equipment a program in electronics should offer. If possible, always take a look for yourself before making a decision about any school.

4. *Ask questions.* What is the school's placement rate for those who have completed programs in electronics? How is it viewed in the community? How do former students feel about it? Does it have a good reputation? Pose questions such as these to school officials, older friends, local businesspersons, or others who may be in a position to know about the school. Such information can be valuable in making an informed choice.

5. *Consider costs.* In making your selection, a major factor should be the cost of attending. Unless money is no issue

with you and your family, it pays to look closely at this matter.

Costs for tuition, fees, and other expenses vary widely from one school to another. In general, the least expensive schools are those considered public institutions because they are funded through tax revenues. For example, public school systems—including not only elementary and secondary education, but also many vocational schools and adult education programs—may be offered free to anyone who can benefit.

Public Two-Year Colleges

The least expensive of the schools that assess tuition tend to be public two-year colleges. Most community, junior, and technical colleges attempt to keep costs as low as possible so that almost anyone can attend. Many two-year colleges charge less than $1,500 for a full academic year. This is very inexpensive when compared with the tuition charged by the typical college or university. In addition, almost all community colleges offer financial aid programs for those who can demonstrate financial need.

Private Schools

It usually costs much more to attend privately owned trade schools and private two-year colleges. Their costs may be much higher than public institutions since they do not receive operating funds from state or local governments. Instead, private schools must rely more on income from tuition and fees charged to students. At trade schools or private colleges, even a short-term program in electronics may cost thousands of dollars to complete. From a dollars-and-cents viewpoint, a public school may make the best choice unless an electronics program is not available in a public school in your area or you believe a private school's quality and reputation are worth the extra investment.

Private schools do enjoy the advantage that their students may receive larger amounts of student aid than those at public institutions. Federal student aid programs calculate awards in part on the cost of attending a given school, meaning that higher aid packages may offset some of the high costs of private schools. Some of these awards may come in the form of loans, however, and they must be paid back over a period of years. So be sure to analyze all related cost factors before enrolling at any school, even if financial aid is available.

Types of Expenses

Expenses that must be paid can include some or all of the following:

- tuition (which may be assessed as a lump sum, a certain amount for each class or each credit hour, or in some other way)

- fees (may be a synonym for tuition or may apply to other costs)
- application fees (often required before enrollment and usually nonrefundable, even if you decide not to attend)
- book costs (not usually charged along with tuition, but they represent an extra cost students must pay, usually to the school's bookstore; may be several hundred dollars for a single term)
- lab fees (often charged to help cover the cost of equipment and supplies)
- activity fees (may be charged even for students who do not participate in recreational or cultural activities)
- health fees (special fees that may be charged to support student health services for all students)
- room and board (may be charged directly by the school or may consist of costs to live off-campus)
- commuting expenses (for students who live at home and commute; can include gasoline, car upkeep, parking fees, bus or train fare, or other expenses)
- other fees (may include costs for taking special tests, technology fees, having transcripts sent to employers or other schools, dropping or adding classes, or other purposes)

By far, the greatest expense is for tuition and basic fees, but it is important not to overlook other costs as well in making educational plans.

OBTAINING FINANCIAL AID

Studying electronics can be expensive, but students who need financial help usually can obtain it. If money is a problem, you could consider applying for financial aid. This can come in the form of a grant, scholarship, loan, work-study award, or other financial assistance.

For most students interested in electronics courses, the best source of aid is the U.S. government. Every year, millions of students receive money from the government through a variety of financial aid programs. Other programs for loans, grants, or scholarships are sponsored at the state level.

To obtain student aid through most government programs, it is necessary to show financial need. The needier you are, the more funding you can expect. At the same time, persons who need help but are not as disadvantaged can qualify for special loans offered at low interest rates.

Other sources of aid include schools and colleges themselves. Many offer a variety of financial aid awards including scholarships, loans, and grants. Also, thousands of private organizations sponsor special aid programs ranging from scholarships to grants.

Students in electronics and other fields will find that a great deal of financial aid is available. The key is to be aggressive in pursuing such assistance. For those willing to fill out forms, meet deadlines, and provide the needed information, chances of receiving financial aid are excellent.

Applying for Aid

The first step in obtaining student aid from the government is to provide information about your family's income, assets, debts, and other financial matters. This is done by completing a detailed application form called the Free Application for Federal Student Aid (FAFSA). You may submit a FAFSA:

- through the Internet by using *FAFSA on the Web*
- by using *FAFSA Express* software, a free software program
- by having your school submit your application electronically
- by mailing a paper FAFSA

You can get a paper FAFSA from your high school or postsecondary school or from the Federal Student Aid Information Center at the following address:

Federal Student Aid Information Center
P.O. Box 84
Washington, DC 20044

You can also obtain these and related forms from high school guidance counselors and from financial aid offices in colleges and trade schools. If you are unsure which form is best for your situation, check with a counselor or financial aid officer.

At first the forms might seem too demanding or even an invasion of privacy, but go ahead and fill one out. If successful, your efforts can lead to a grant, loan, or other assistance worth thousands of dollars.

In this process, make certain you meet application deadlines. The best time to apply is around January 1 of the calendar year in which you plan to begin your autumn postsecondary studies. In other words, this is eight or nine months before you begin school. Since some federal programs award money on a first-come, first-served basis, the earlier an application is submitted, the better. At any rate, make certain you apply before May 1 for fall enrollment.

Types of Financial Aid Available

The government sponsors several types of aid programs. Following is a brief overview of major awards available. Keep in mind that many students receive a package of aid consisting of several different types of awards.

PELL GRANTS

Pell Grants are designed for students who have genuine financial need. Many people consider them the most desirable type of award available. After all, a grant does not have to be repaid—ever!

The amount any one student receives will vary according to individual finances, costs at the school being attended, and related factors. Recent students have received anywhere from a few hundred dollars to well over $2,000 yearly, and the upper limit is being raised to an even higher amount. This award is based on need, not grades or other academic factors.

The major appeal of this type of grant is that if you really need one, you are almost certain to receive it if you apply properly. This means that financial limitations should not keep you from pursuing a career in electronics.

SUPPLEMENTAL EDUCATIONAL OPPORTUNITY GRANTS (SEOG)

Supplemental Educational Opportunity Grants (SEOG) are much like Pell Grants, but not as many awards are available each year. They, too, need not be repaid. Since overall funds are limited, it is very important to apply early if you hope to land one of these grants.

LOAN OPTIONS

Government-sponsored loan programs provide another set of options. Some are offered by the government itself, while others come from private lending agencies with government backing. They must be repaid after your education is completed, but most offer a long time to repay as well as lower interest rates than ordinary commercial loans.

One of the most popular loan programs is the Perkins Loan program. This provides loans with relatively low interest rates and plenty of time to repay the loan.

Another widely used program is the Stafford Loan program, which offers similar benefits. The Stafford is different, however, in that such loans are obtained directly from a bank, credit union, or other financial institution. Interest rates are lower than conventional loans thanks to government backing of the loans.

Other loans that place less emphasis on financial need also are available. Many families have incomes that are too high for need-based programs, but a loan still would be helpful in meeting educational expenses. For such situations, PLUS loans or SLS loans (Supplemental Loans for Students) offer an attractive alternative. PLUS loans are made directly to parents of students, while SLS are taken out by students. Both types of loans are made through banks or other private lenders, and the major requirement is a good credit rating.

Work-Study

Some students earn money to apply to school expenses through the College Work-Study Program, where students hold part-time jobs at their college or a cooperating agency. Typical jobs include working in a dean's office, staffing the switchboard, serving as a lab assistant, or helping out in the college's library, bookstore, or grounds crew.

Participants in this program earn at least the federal minimum wage. They also gain job experience, which can be helpful in showing prospective employers that they have been successful workers, as well as the chance to receive letters of recommendation from college staff members who have served as work-study supervisors.

Additional Aid Possibilities

Other sources of student aid may be available in addition to those offered by the government. For example, consider possibilities such as these:

- scholarships and grants offered by individual schools
- grants or scholarships offered by professional associations related to electronics
- scholarships sponsored by organizations to which you or a parent belong, such as churches or civic clubs
- tuition programs sponsored by companies for their employees (a great possibility if you can gain employment before completing an educational program or wish to move up from one level to another)

ALTERNATIVE TRAINING PROGRAMS

In addition to electronics programs offered by schools and colleges, other training options also exist. These include apprenticeships, informal on-the-job training, and special training programs offered by employers.

Apprenticeship Programs

One effective way to learn a craft or trade is to serve as an apprentice. This involves working under the guidance of experienced workers in the field being studied.

Apprenticeships represent one of the oldest forms of training in existence. They became common during the Middle Ages, when workers learned the basics of a trade or craft by serving as apprentices to persons with skills gained from years of experience. Although less common today, now that we benefit from the availability of so many schools, apprenticeships still offer a valid alternative method of training.

Modern apprenticeship programs may be offered by companies, labor unions, or a combination of the two. For electronics technicians, it usually takes three or four years to complete an apprenticeship. An advantage over most other training programs is that participants are paid while they participate. The rate of pay is lower than for fully qualified workers, but it usually is raised as skills are acquired.

Serving as an apprentice is a time-honored tradition. It offers a detailed, methodical method of learning from experienced workers while gaining and maintaining employment. If you are interested in such an opportunity, check with employers in your area to see if apprenticeships are offered and how you might become involved.

On-the-Job Training and Company Training Programs

Another approach for learning about electronics is to participate in a company-sponsored training program. Some of these opportunities consist of very informal on-the-job training. Others may include structured classes, which may cover material similar to that taught in schools but usually condensed over a shorter time period. The main advantages of company programs are that no cost is involved (employees may even be paid to attend) and training can be finished rapidly.

Information about company training programs can be obtained from the personnel office of firms that employ electronics technicians and related workers. Announcements of such opportunities also may appear in newspapers or other publications.

CHAPTER 8

EARNINGS AND BENEFITS

EARNINGS

Men and women who pursue careers in electronics can earn good wages and fringe benefits. The actual amounts vary widely depending on the type of job performed and a number of other factors. But in general, persons employed in this field earn significantly more than unskilled workers and many skilled workers employed in nontechnical fields. Following are some examples of salaries and wages that can be expected in this field.

According to the U.S. Department of Labor, full-time electronic equipment repairers had a median weekly income of $619 in 1996. This meant that half earned above this amount and half earned less. The top salaries exceeded $979 per week, or more than $50,000 per year.

Median annual salaries in different job categories were as follows:

telephone installers and repairers: $37,284
electronic repairers, communications and industrial equipment: $31,304

office machine repairers: $30,264
data processing equipment repairers: $29,796

Beginning wages vary widely depending on the employer, the region of the country, and other factors. Starting wages of $10 to $15 an hour were common in 1998. Some high-tech manufacturers are now offering beginning salaries of $30,000 to $50,000 yearly in specialized areas such as semiconductor manufacturing, according to SEMATECH, a consortium of semiconductor manufacturers.

Engineers working in electronics earn even higher salaries. According to the Institute of Electrical and Electronics Engineers, U.S. professionals in electrical, electronic, and computer engineering who were members of this organization had a median income of $72,000 in 1997, with an average salary increase of several percent each year.

It is important to note that wages and salaries vary not only from one type of job to another, but within similar job categories. A number of factors can influence remuneration, including the following:

Educational level. In general, positions requiring a greater level of educational preparation pay higher salaries. An engineer with a bachelor's or master's degree, for instance, usually will earn more than a technician with two years or fewer of postsecondary training.

Location. Workers in large cities tend to make more than those in rural areas, and those in areas with a higher cost of living usually earn higher wages. For example, housing, food, and other fundamentals tend to cost much more in Boston or Los Angeles than in rural Montana or Alabama. Thus workers in all categories, including electronics, usually demand correspondingly higher salaries and wages.

Economic trends. During times of inflation, salaries and wages tend to go up. When the regional or national economy slows down, on the other hand, raises may be smaller or nonexistent for a while.

Skill and experience. An experienced technician or other electronics worker generally earns more than one with little or no experience. This is always the case in union environments, where apprentices or other new workers must strive to achieve journeyman status. Things might not be as extensively formalized in nonunion settings, but here, too, experienced workers tend to earn more.

Job competition. Competition among companies that employ workers in electronics is often a factor in earning potential. For example, if one firm raises its salaries, another employer in the same city may feel compelled to do the same to avoid having workers leave for better paying jobs. On the other hand, a lack of such competition may help keep salaries at a lower-than-average level.

Employer status. A new business that is struggling to establish itself may not be able to pay as well as one that has flourished for years. Similarly, one that hires only union members may have a higher wage scale than a nonunion operation.

BENEFITS

Along with salaries or wages, most employers provide several types of benefits to their employees. Benefits vary from one company to another and are usually more extensive for full-time employees than for part-timers. In some cases, the total amount paid in benefits can be more than 30 percent of the base salary. This can be a significant factor in making a decision about whether to accept a job offer.

Typically such benefits include the following:

- health insurance
- retirement funds
- paid sick leave
- paid vacations
- worker's compensation in case of injury
- Social Security benefits

In addition, employees in some companies enjoy the added benefit of participating in profit-sharing programs, where they may own stock in the company or obtain bonuses based on the company's overall performance. Other possible benefits include extra medical coverage (such as dental or optical insurance), life insurance, performance bonuses, and other benefits.

In considering any employment situation, it is important to learn what benefits are available before making a decision to accept the job. The total package of salaries or wages *and* fringe benefits should be reviewed when considering one job against another, not just earnings alone.

CHAPTER 9

ELECTRONICS ORGANIZATIONS AND CERTIFICATIONS

A common stereotype in the movies and on television is that of the basement inventor, who labors alone on special projects accompanied by flashing lights, various electronic devices, and other esoteric trappings. But few people in engineering or other technological jobs actually work in isolation. Most men and women who work in electronics coordinate their activities closely with others who perform similar functions. In addition to cooperating in the workplace, many hold membership in special groups related to their professional interests. Such organizations include labor unions, professional societies focusing on different areas of electronics, and other organizations.

ADVANTAGES OF MEMBERSHIPS

Participation in an electronics organization can be highly worthwhile. The benefits provided to members range from the sharing of useful information to the sponsorship of special programs to certify technical competency.

Professional Electronics Technicians Association (ETA)

The Professional Electronics Technicians Association (ETA) lists six reasons technicians should find membership beneficial:

1. improvement of pay and prestige through group efforts
2. monthly information on various phases of electronics, including circuit descriptions and short quizzes
3. business seminars and other management information for those who are service managers
4. discounts on trade magazines, technical books, and other items
5. opportunities for people with common interests to get together and share information
6. a certification program

This association, based in Greencastle, Indiana, welcomes memberships from individual technicians, electronics students, and owners of businesses and institutions, among others. Annual membership fees range from $20 for students to $125 for institutions (some schools, for instance, hold membership in this organization). In addition to regular ETA membership, each member may participate in one of the following divisions:

- educators
- certified technicians
- Canadian division
- communication techs
- medical
- industrial
- shop owners

International Society of
Certified Electronics Technicians

A similar organization is the International Society of Certified Electronics Technicians, which has its national headquarters in Ft. Worth, Texas. Its functions include direction and administration of:

1. the Certified Electronics Technician (CET) program
2. a national apprenticeship and training program
3. technical information training and upgrading programs
4. serviceability inspection programs

Originating as an offshoot of the National Electronic Association in 1970, this organization currently has more than twenty-eight thousand members. To be eligible for membership, an electronics technician must have passed the organization's CET exam. Once membership is conferred, men and women benefit from not only the information and networking provided, but also the stature of having passed a recognized certification process.

Other Organizations

Persons employed in electronics jobs other than as technicians may elect to participate in other organizations. Owners of their own electronics repair firms, for example, may join a group such as the National Electronic Sales and Service Dealers Association. Engineers may join an organization for engineers from a variety of fields, or join one that is more specialized, such as the Institute of Electrical and Electronics Engineers.

LABOR UNIONS

Many persons employed in electronics belong to labor unions. These organizations allow workers to join together to promote the welfare of members of the group, especially in terms of their relations with employers. Unions have been a major force in American and Canadian business and industry for more than a hundred years. A number of advancements—such as shorter work weeks, higher pay, fringe benefits, and expanded worker rights—have resulted from the efforts of labor unions.

Men and women employed in electronics jobs may belong to a number of unions, including the following:

1. International Brotherhood of Electrical Workers
2. International Union of Electronic, Electrical, Salaried, Machine and Furniture Workers

3. United Electrical, Radio and Machine Workers of America
4. Federation of Westinghouse Independent Salaried Unions

Some of the benefits offered by labor unions include:

- apprentice training opportunities
- guaranteed wage levels and other benefits provided by the employer in accordance with contracts negotiated by union representatives
- voting rights, such as the right to vote for union officials and the right to vote for or against proposed contracts
- informative publications for members
- pension plans and other benefits managed by the union for its members
- protection against unfair labor practices
- strength in numbers, which helps counterbalance the power employers can hold over their employees

Labor unions depend on dues from members to sustain their operations. This means that as a member, you must pay a specified amount each month or pay period toward these costs. A typical amount for dues is a contribution of the equivalent of two hours' wages per month, although this can vary. For a large union with thousands of members, overall income can be significant. This money is then used to support a wide range of union activities to improve wages, working conditions, and other employment-related matters.

At any given time, a labor union might be lobbying Congress in support of legislation that would have a positive impact on its members, negotiating with employers for a new contract, sponsoring a scholarship program for children of union members, or working to improve members' medical benefits.

In the electronics field, union membership is more common with employees of large firms than it is with smaller companies such as one- or two-person repair businesses. It also is more typical of urban areas than rural ones and in certain geographical locations. The southern United States, for example, is not a strong union region compared to the northern United States and parts of Canada.

In some settings, union membership is virtually required. Elsewhere, it may be entirely up to the individual. In any case, many persons employed in electronics-related jobs find union membership beneficial.

CERTIFICATIONS

How can you prove to a prospective employer or customer that you are qualified to repair electronic equipment or perform other work in electronics? Holding a diploma or degree in an electronics field is one good indicator of competence. Another is to become certified through a nationally recognized certification process.

Electronics Technicians Association Certification

Electronics technicians and students of electronics can become certified through organizations such as those discussed earlier in this chapter. The Electronics Technicians Association, for example, sponsors an examination process leading to one of the following designations:

Associate. The exam at this level is offered to students and to technicians with fewer than four years of experience.

Journeyman. This level is designed for technicians with at least four years of experience and/or education in electronics. The exam includes the basic electronics information required for associates, as well as an option of the student's choice.

Senior. Requiring eight years of experience, this level also requires a higher passage rate than the journeyman designation.

Master. Technicians with at least eight years of experience who can demonstrate competency in six major electronics categories can earn this level of recognition.

Categories and specialty areas in which students can be tested include the following:

Category: Consumer Electronics
           Specialty areas: Radio/TV, VCR, Sound
Category: Video Distribution
           Specialty areas: MATV, Antenna, Satellite

Category: Telecommunications
         Specialty areas: Phone, Data, Microwave, VSAT
Category: Industrial
Category: Computer
Category: Biomedical

Students and technicians take these certification exams at a variety of locations around the United States and Canada, including schools, colleges, and other locations. Those in the military can sit for the exams at military bases around the world. Upon passing, technicians receive certificates and become registered with the Electronics Technicians Association as certified engineering technicians (CETs). This can prove valuable in many ways, ranging from intangible benefits such as increased self-confidence, to tangible proof of competencies needed to obtain a job or promotion.

International Society of Certified Electronics Technicians

Another certification process is sponsored by the International Society of Certified Electronics Technicians. More than twenty-eight thousand men and women currently hold certification from this organization. The association sponsors examinations that can lead to one of two certification levels: associate or journeyman.

The associate-level exam may be taken by students or by technicians with fewer than four years of experience in the field. The journeyman-level exam is open only to those who have four years of experience or more. It includes not only a basic electronic portion, but also components in special fields of electronics chosen by the individual taking the exam. Those who pass either exam benefit from the recognition involved in this highly reputable process.

If you plan to work as a technician, taking one or more certification exams is well worth considering. Certification credentials can be a valuable asset for one's entire professional life.

CHAPTER 10

GETTING STARTED

Now that you have reviewed the information provided in previous chapters, does a career in electronics seem to match your own interests and abilities? Can you see yourself working as an electronics technician or engineer, or in some other position in the field? If so, the next step is to make concrete plans for pursuing such a career, and then follow up on them.

TAKING THE FIRST STEPS

Here are seven basic steps you might take to get started in the direction of an electronics career:

1. If you are still in high school, take any related courses that are available. For example, most physics courses provide information needed to understand the basic concepts and theories behind electronics. If vocational classes are offered, you might complete an

introductory electronics class, even if you plan to pursue postsecondary training in the field. That way, you can gain some hands-on experience in working with electronics devices.

2. In addition to high school courses, other kinds of training programs may be available to you. If you are still in high school, don't wait until graduation or late in your senior year to do this, but try to plan ahead. If you are an adult who has completed—or dropped out of—school, why put things off any longer? Go ahead and start looking around now for the training that can improve your future.

3. Once you decide what kind of program and school seem best for you (for example, a community college or a trade school), fill out admission applications or any other required forms.

4. Apply for financial aid if you need such assistance.

5. Once you are admitted, go to class, apply yourself, and earn a diploma or degree in an electronics field.

6. If you prefer an alternative approach, apply for a job with a firm that offers its own on-the-job training program or cooperates in offering an apprenticeship program. Then work diligently to complete the program.

7. Remember the importance of credentials. When you gain credentials, which indicate you are qualified to work in electronics, you can be on your way to a successful career!

GETTING A JOB

The next step after gaining educational credentials is to locate a job for which you are qualified. This may happen quickly and easily, or it may take weeks or months of effort. Because of the demand for workers in electronics, most persons with the right qualifications should have less difficulty in obtaining a job than do those in many other fields. At any rate, the process requires initiative. It is up to you to find out about job vacancies and then pursue them.

Identifying Job Vacancies

One of the best places to locate job openings is the classified section of any newspaper. This is particularly true of daily papers serving larger towns and cities.

Following is a representative classified ad that appeared in the *Washington Post*.

ELECTRONIC TECH. Candidate will be responsible for repair and maintenance of electronic security systems consisting of microprocessor and PLC based locking control systems, CCTV systems, perimeter security systems, intercom systems, etc. Positions available in several cities. Allow for travel in U.S. Experience in field service or electronic security desired. Will consider recent electronic or EE graduate. An Equal Opportunity Employer.

In addition, companies planning to hire new or replacement workers often post job announcements on bulletin boards or in other public places. Any firm's human resources officer or personnel office also will provide this information on request.

Another source of job information is your local employment service or job service office. These offices are supported by state or local governments to provide assistance in locating jobs.

A school or college you have attended also should provide assistance in job searches. To obtain help, contact the school's placement office or career counselor.

Doing Well in Job Interviews

A standard procedure in seeking a job is filling out a written job application. If this is required, be sure to do the following:

1. Take your time in filling out the form.
2. Answer all questions completely and honestly.
3. Be as neat as possible. If time and circumstances allow, type the application. If this is not possible, write neatly and legibly. Use a pen, not a pencil, and remember that you are trying to make a good impression.
4. Check your work closely for errors in spelling or grammar.

5. Prepare a neatly typed resume in advance, and attach it to applications or use it instead of application forms, if allowed.
6. For persons you list as a reference, make certain you have contacted them in advance to (a) get their permission for such usage, and (b) make sure they will be prepared to give you a positive recommendation.

If you are lucky, a completed application will be followed by a job interview. It is here that most jobs are won or lost, with the written application serving only to get you to this stage. To do your best in interviews, take measures such as these:

1. Be on time. Lateness only makes a bad impression, and it may cost you the job.
2. Avoid being too eager. Even if you think you need the job badly, try not to show it. A calm, professional manner works best. Act interested, but not desperate.
3. Dress neatly. Appearances do count, so make sure you wear clean, neat clothes.
4. Engage in a two-way conversation. Although it is the interviewer's job to ask most of the questions, ask some questions of your own. These should dwell on the nature of the job, not on issues such as wages and benefits, which can be discussed in more detail if you are offered the job. Show that you are interested and capable of asking intelligent questions.

Will your interview lead to a job? One never knows in any given situation. But it only takes one success! Then you can begin working in the electronics field, with all the potential such a move holds for a truly interesting career.

BIBLIOGRAPHY

Baxter, Neale. "A Positive Connection: Electronics and Careers." *Occupational Outlook Quarterly.* Winter 1989–90, 16–27.

"The CET Exam." International Society of Certified Electronics Technicians.

Chirico, Joann. *Career Portraits: Electronics.* Lincolnwood, IL: NTC/Contemporary Publishing Group, Inc., 1995.

Christianson, Donald. *Electronic Engineers Handbook.* New York: McGraw-Hill, 1994.

Engineer's Guide to Lifelong Employability. Piscataway, NJ: Institute of Electrical and Electronics Engineers, 1997.

"How to Join ETA." Professional Electronics Technicians Association.

Lahue, Fabian. *Electronic Troubleshooting.* New York: McGraw-Hill, 1994.

Malvino, Albert Paul. *Electronic Principles.* New York: McGraw Hill, 1994.

Rowh, Mark. *Opportunities in Installation and Repair Careers.* Lincolnwood, IL: NTC/Contemporary Publishing Group, Inc., 1994.

U.S. Department of Labor. *Dictionary of Occupational Titles.* 1991.

U.S. Department of Labor. *Occupational Outlook Handbook.* 1998.

"Your Career in the Electrical, Electronics, and Computer Engineering Fields." Institute of Electrical and Electronics Engineers.

SELECTED ORGANIZATIONS RELATED TO ELECTRONICS

American Electronics Association
  5201 Great American Parkway, Suite 520
  Santa Clara, CA 95054

Canadian Academy of Engineering
  130 Albert Street
  Ottawa, Ontario K1P 5G4

Canadian Society for Engineering Management
  250 Consumers Road, Suite 201
  Willodale, Ontario M2J 4V6

Electronic Industries Association
  2500 Wilson Boulevard
  Arlington, VA 22201

The Electronics Technicians Association, International
  602 North Jackson Street
  Greencastle, IN 46135

International Federation of Professional and Technical
    Engineers
  8630 Fenton Street
  Silver Spring, MD 20910

International Society of Certified Electronics Technicians
  2708 West Berry Street
  Fort Worth, TX 76109

International Union of Electronic, Electrical, Salaried,
    Machine and Furniture Workers
  1126 Sixteenth Street, NW
  Washington, DC 20036

National Electronic Service Dealers
  2708 West Berry Street
  Ft. Worth, TX 76109

United States Telephone Association
  1401 H Street NW, Suite 600
  Washington, DC 20005

TRADE AND TECHNICAL SCHOOLS OFFERING ELECTRONICS PROGRAMS

The following private trade and technical schools are just some of those offering instructional programs in electronics.

Alabama

Herzing College of Business & Technology
280 West Valley Avenue
Homewood, AL 35209

ITT Technical Institute
500 Riverhills Business Park
Birmingham, AL 35242

Southeast College of Technology
828 Downtowner Loop West
Mobile, AL 36609

Arizona

High Tech Institute
1515 East Indian School Road
Phoenix, AZ 85014

ITT Technical Institute
1840 East Benson Highway
Tucson, AZ 85714

ITT Technical Institute
4837 East McDowell Road
Phoenix, AZ 85008

Arkansas

ITT Technical Institute
4520 South University
Little Rock, AR 72209

California

Golden State School
1690 Universe Circle
Oxnard, CA 93033

ITT Technical Institute
2035 East 233rd Street
Carson, CA 90810

ITT Technical Institute
2051 Solar Drive
Oxnard, CA 93030

ITT Technical Institute
9700 Goethe Road
Sacramento, CA 95287

ITT Technical Institute
 9680 Granite Ridge Drive
 San Diego, CA 92123

ITT Technical Institute
 12669 Ecinitas Avenue
 Sylmar, CA 91342

ITT Technical Institute
 1530 West Cameron Avenue
 West Corvina, CA 91790

Los Angeles ORT Technical Institute
 635 South Harvard Boulevard
 Los Angeles, CA 90005

Practical Schools
 900 East Ball Road
 Anaheim, CA 92805

School of Communication Electronics
 184 Second Street
 San Francisco, CA 94105

Southern California Institute of Technology
 1900 West Crescent Avenue
 Anaheim, CA 92801

Colorado

Control Data Institute
 720 South Colorado Boulevard
 Denver, CO 80222

Denver Institute of Technology
  7350 North Broadway
  Denver, CO 80221

Technical Trades Institute
  772 Horizon Drive
  Grand Junction, CO 81506

Connecticut

Connecticut School of Electronics
  586 Grasso Boulevard
  New Haven, CT 06519

Porter and Chester Institute
  138 Weymouth Street
  Enfield, CT 06082

Porter and Chester Institute
  670 Lordship Boulevard
  Stratford, CT 06497

Delaware

Star Technical Institute
  631 West Newport Pike
  Wilmington, DE 19802

Florida

ATI Career Training Center
  1 NE Nineteenth Street
  Miami, Florida 33132

ITT Technical Institute
  7955 NW Twelfth Street
  Miami, FL 33126

ITT Technical Institute
  4809 Memorial Highway
  Tampa, FL 33634

Hawaii

Electronics Institute
  1270 Queen Emma Street
  Honolulu, HI 96813

Illinois

Coyne American Institute
  1235 West Fullerton Avenue
  Chicago, IL 60614

ITT Technical Institute
  375 West Higgins Road
  Hoffman Estates, IL 60195

Indiana

ITT Technical Institute
  4919 Coldwater Road
  Fort Wayne, IN 46825

ITT Technical Institute
  9511 Angola Court
  Indianapolis, IN 46268

Iowa

Hamilton Technical College
  1011 East Fifty-third Street
  Davenport, IA 52807

Kansas

Topeka Technical College
  1620 NW Gage Boulevard
  Topeka, KS 66618

Wichita Technical Institute
  942 South West Street
  Wichita, KS 67213

Kentucky

Institute of Electronics Technology
  509 South Thirtieth Street
  Paducah, KY 42001

Louisville Technical Institute
  3901 Atkinson Drive
  Louisville, KY 40218

RETS Electronic Institute
  300 High Rise Drive
  Louisville, KY 40213

Louisiana

Education America-Southeast College of Technology
  3321 Hessmer Avenue
  Metairie, LA 70002

ITT Technical College
  13944 Airline Highway
  Baton Rouge, LA 70817

Maryland

RETS Technical Training Center
  1520 South Caton Avenue
  Baltimore, MD 21227

TESST Technology Institute
  5122 Baltimore Avenue
  Hyattsville, MD 20781

Massachusetts

Northeast Institute of Industrial Technology
  41 Phillips Street
  Boston, MA 02114

Porter and Chester Institute
  134 Dulong Circle
  Chicopee, MA 01022

Michigan

ITT Technical Institute
  4020 Sparks Drive SE
  Grand Rapids, MI 49546

National Institute of Technology
  26555 Evergreen
  Southfield, MI 48076

Minnesota

Dunwoody Industrial Institute
  818 Dunwoody Boulevard
  Minneapolis, MN 55403

NEI College of Technology
  825 Forty-first Avenue NE
  Columbia Heights, MN 55421

Missouri

Missouri Technical School
  1167 Corporate Lake Drive
  St. Louis, MO 63132

TAD Technical Institute
  7910 Troost Avenue
  Kansas City, MO 64131

Nebraska

ITT Technical Institute
  9814 M Street
  Omaha, NE 68127

New Jersey

Lincoln Technical Institute
  Haddonfield Road at Route 130N
  Pennsauken, NJ 08110

Metropolitan Technical Institute
  11 Daniel Road
  Fairfield, NJ 07004

New York

Island Drafting and Technical Institute
  128 Broadway
  Amityville, NY 11701

ITT Technical Institute
  2295 Millersport Highway
  Getzville, NY 14068

Suburban Technical School
  175 Fulton Avenue
  Hempstead, NY 11550

Ohio

Bryant and Stratton College
  1700 East Thirteenth Street
  Cleveland, OH 44114

ETI Technical College of Niles
  2076-86 Youngstown-Warren Road
  Niles, OH 44446

Remington College
  1445 Broadway Avenue
  Cleveland, OH 44125

Total Technical Institute
  6500 Pearl Road
  Parma Heights, OH 44130

Oklahoma

NEC-Spartan School of Aeronautics
  8820 East Pine Street
  Tulsa, OK 74158

Oregon

ITT Technical Institute
  6035 NE Seventy-eighth Court
  Portland, OR 97218

Pennsylvania

Erie Institute of Technology
2221 Peninsula Drive
Erie, PA 16506

Johnson Technical Institute
3427 North Main Avenue
Scranton, PA 18508

Lincoln Technical Institute
5151 Tildham Street
Allentown, PA 18104

Pennco Tech
3815 Otter Street
Bristol, PA 19007

Philadelphia Wireless Technical Institute
1531-33 Pine Street
Philadelphia, PA 19102

Pittsburgh Institute of Aeronautics
P.O. Box 10897
Pittsburgh, PA 15236

York Technical Institute
1405 Williams Road
York, PA 17402

Rhode Island

New England Technical College
  2500 Post Road
  Warwick, RI 02886

Tennessee

ITT Technical Institute
  441 Donelson Pike
  Nashville, TN 37214

Tennessee Institute of Electronics
  3202 Tazewell Pike
  Knoxville, TN 37918

Texas

ATI-American Trades Institute
  6627 Maple Avenue
  Dallas, TX 75235

Hallmark Institute of Technology
  10401 IH10 West
  San Antonio, TX 78230

National Institute of Technology
  3622 Fredericksburg Road
  San Antonio, TX 78201

Southwest School of Electronics
  5424 Highway 290 West
  Austin, TX 78735

Western Technical Institute
1000 Texas Avenue
El Paso, TX 79901

Virginia

ITT Technical Institute
863 Glenrock Road
Norfolk, VA 23502

TESST Technology Institute
1400 Duke Street
Alexandria, VA 22314

Washington

ITT Technical Institute
12720 Gateway Drive
Seattle, WA 98168

West Virginia

National Institute of Technology
5514 Big Tyler Road
Cross Lanes, WV 25313

Wisconsin

ITT Technical Institute
6300 West Layton Avenue
Greenfield, WI 53220

Canada

CDI College of Business & Technology
#218, 9402-135 Avenue
Northwood Mall
Edmonton, AB T5E 5R8

CDI College of Business & Technology
Burlington Square, 5172 Kingsway
Burnaby, BC V5H 2E8

CompuCollege School of Business
#210-5021 Kingsway, Marlborough Court
Burnaby, BC V5H 4A5

Greater Regional Technical College
847 Fisgard Street
Victoria, BC V8W 1R9

Ridge Meadows Business & Career Training Centre
Maple Ridge Secondary School, 21911-122nd Avenue
Maple Ridge, BC V2X 3X2

Herzing Career College
723 Portage Avenue
Winnipeg, MB R3G 0M8

CompuCollege School of Business
One Court Manche, P.O. Box 1690, Station 'B'
Happy Valley-Goose Bay, LB A0P 1E0

The Career Academy
  P.O. Box 71
  Corner Brook, NF A2H 6C3

CompuCollege School of Business
  1526 Dresden Row, P.O. Box 3608
  Halifax, NS B3J 3K6

CDI College of Business & Technology
  2 King Street West
  Jackson Square, Plaza Level
  Hamilton, ON L8P 1A1

RETS Career Training
  2057 Danforth Avenue, Suite 200
  Toronto, ON M4C 1J8

Toronto School of Business
  212-359 Bayfield Street
  Barrie, ON L4M 3C3

APPENDIX C

TWO-YEAR COLLEGES OFFERING PROGRAMS IN ELECTRONICS

In addition to trade schools, many two-year colleges offer programs in electronics. Junior, community, and technical colleges can be found throughout the United States and Canada, with most serving a local region from which students commute to classes. Many, but not all, of these colleges offer programs in electronics. Consult any college's catalog or contact its admissions office to find out if electronics programs are available.

A partial listing of colleges offering electronics follows. If your local community college is not listed, that does not necessarily mean that it does not offer electronics. For any college in which you are interested, contact the institution directly to make sure.

Alabama

Gadsden State Community College
Gadsden, AL 35999

George C. Wallace State Community College
Dothan, AL 36303

Jefferson State Community College
Birmingham, AL 35215

John C. Calhoun State Community College
Decatur, AL 35609

Arizona

Arizona Western College
Yuma, AZ 85364

Cochise College
Douglas, AZ 85607

Eastern Arizona College
Thatcher, AZ 85552

Glendale Community College
Glendale, AZ 85302

Northland Pioneer College
Holbrook, AZ 86025

Phoenix College
Phoenix, AZ 85013

Pima Community College
Tucson, AZ 85709

Rio Salado Community College
  Phoenix, AZ 85003

Yavapai College
  Prescott, AZ 86301

Arkansas

Arkansas State University—Beebe Branch
  Beebe, AR 72012

East Arkansas Community College
  Forrest City, AR 72335

Garland County Community College
  Hot Springs, AR 71913

Mississippi County Community College
  Blytheville, AR 72316

Phillips County Community College
  Helena, AR 72342

Westark Community College
  Fort Smith, AR 72913

California

Cabrillo College
  Aptos, CA 95003

Chabot College
  Hayward, CA 94545

Chaffey Community College
  Rancho Cucamonga, CA 91701

College of the Redwoods
  Eureka, CA 95501

Cosumnes River College
  Sacramento, CA 95823

Cuyamaca College
  El Cajon, CA 92019

Fullerton College
  Fullerton, CA 92634

Golden West College
  Huntington Beach, CA 92647

Los Angeles City College
  Los Angeles, CA 90029

Los Angeles Pierce College
  Woodland Hills, CA 91371

Mission College
  Santa Clara, CA 95054

Mt. San Antonio College
  Walnut, CA 91789

Mt. San Jacinto College
  San Jacinto, CA 92383

Napa Valley College
Napa, CA 94558

Orange Coast College
Costa Mesa, CA 92626

Rancho Santiago Community College
Santa Ana, CA 92706

Santa Rosa Junior College
Santa Rosa, CA 95401

Yuba College
Marysville, CA 95901

Colorado

Aims Community College
Greeley, CO 80631

Community College of Aurora
Aurora, CO 80011

Front Range Community College
Westminster, CO 80030

Morgan Community College
Ft. Morgan, CO 80701

Northeastern Junior College
Sterling, CO 80751

Pikes Peak Community College
Colorado Springs, CO 80906

Pueblo Community College
  Pueblo, CO 81004

Red Rocks Community College
  Lakewood, CO 80228

Connecticut

Norwalk State Technical College
  Norwalk, CT 06854

Florida

Brevard Community College
  Cocoa, FL 32922

Indian River Community College
  Fort Pierce, FL 34981

Lake City Community College
  Lake City, FL 32055

Manatee Community College
  Bradenton, FL 32406

Miami-Dade Community College
  Miami, FL 33132

Palm Beach Community College
  Lake Worth, FL 33461

Santa Fe Community College
  Gainesville, FL 32606

Seminole Community College
  Sanford, FL 32773

Georgia

Coastal Georgia Community College
  Brunswick, GA 31520

Gainesville College
  Gainesville, GA 30503

Middle Georgia College
  Cochran, GA 31014

Hawaii

University of Hawaii—Hawaii Community College
  Hilo, HI 96720

University of Hawaii—Honolulu Community College
  Honolulu, HI 96817

University of Hawaii—Kauai Community College
  Lihue, HI 96766

Idaho

Eastern Idaho Technical College
  Idaho Falls, ID 83404

North Idaho College
  Coeur D'Alene, ID 83814

Illinois

Belleville Area College
  Belleville, IL 62221

Black Hawk College
  Moline, IL 61265

College of Du Page
  Glen Ellyn, IL 60137

Elgin Community College
  Elgin, IL 60123

Highland Community College
  Freeport, IL 61032

Joliet Junior College
  Joliet, IL 60431

Kennedy-King College
  Chicago, IL 60621

Kishwaukee College
  Malta, IL 60150

Lewis and Clark Community College
  Godfrey, IL 62035

McHenry County College
  Crystal Lake, IL 60012

Moraine Valley Community College
  Palos Hills, IL 60465

Richard J. Daley College
    Chicago, IL 60652

Rock Valley College
    Rockford, IL 61114

Shawnee Community College
    Ullin, IL 62992

Southeastern Illinois College
    Harrisburg, IL 62946

Triton College
    River Grove, IL 60171

Wabash Valley College
    Mt. Carmel, IL 62863

William Rainey Harper College
    Palatine, IL 60067

Iowa

Clinton Community College
    Clinton, IA 52732

Iowa Central Community College
    Fort Dodge, IA 50501

Iowa Western Community College
    Council Bluffs, IA 51503

Kirkwood Community College
    Cedar Rapids, IA 52406

Northwest Iowa Community College
Sheldon, IA 51201

Western Iowa Technical Community College
Sioux City, IA 51102

Kansas

Allen County Community College
Iola, KS 66749

Butler County Community College
El Dorado, KS 67042

Cowley County Community College
Arkansas City, KS 67005

Garden City Community College
Garden City, KS 67846

Haskell Indian Nations University
Lawrence, KS 66046

Johnson County Community College
Overland Park, KS 66210

Kansas City Kansas Community College
Kansas City, KS 66112

Neosho County Community College
Chanute, KS 66720

Kentucky

Maysville Community College
Maysville, KY 41956

Owensboro Community College
Owensboro, KY 42303

Maryland

Catonsville Community College
Baltimore, MD 21228

Dundalk Community College
Dundalk, MD 21222

Frederick Community College
Frederick, MD 21702

Massachusetts

Massasoit Community College
Brockton, MA 02402

Middlesex Community College
Bedford, MA 01730

Springfield Technical Community College
Springfield, MA 01105

Michigan

Alpena Community College
Alpena, MI 49707

Delta College
  University Center, MI 48710

Gogebic Community College
  Ironwood, MI 49938

Henry Ford Community College
  Dearborn, MI 48128

Kellogg Community College
  Battle Creek, MI 49017

Macomb County Community College
  Warren, MI 48093

Northwestern Michigan College
  Traverse City, MI 49684

Oakland Community College
  Bloomfield Hills, MI 48013

Schoolcraft College
  Livonia, MI 48152

West Shore Community College
  Scottville, MI 49454

Minnesota

Anoka-Ramsey Community College
  Coon Rapids, MN 55433

Lakewood Community College
  White Bear Lake, MN 55110

North Hennepin Community College
  Brooklyn Park, MN 55445

Wilmar Technical College
  Wilmar, MN 56201

Mississippi

East Central Junior College
  Decatur, MS 39327

Hinds Community College
  Raymond, MS 39154

Holmes Community College
  Goodman, MS 39079

Itawamba Community College
  Fulton, MS 38843

Jones County Junior College
  Ellisville, MS 39437

Mississippi Delta Community College
  Moorhead, MS 38761

Mississippi Gulf Coast Community College
  Perkinston, MS 39573

Pearl River Community College
  Poplarville, MS 39470

Missouri

East Central College
   Union, MO 63084

Maple Woods Community College
   Kansas City, MO 64156

Moberly Area Junior College
   Moberly, MO 65270

St. Louis Community College
   St. Louis, MO 63102

Nebraska

Central Community College, Platte Campus
   Columbus, NE 68601

Mid-Plains Community College
   North Platte, NE 69101

Northeast Community College
   Norfolk, NE 68702

Western Nebraska Community College
   Sidney, NE 69162

Nevada

Great Basin Community College
   Elko, NV 89801

Truckee Meadows Community College
   Reno, NV 89512

Western Nevada Community College
   Carson City, NV 89703

New Hampshire

New Hampshire Community Technical College
   Berlin, NH 03102

New Jersey

Atlantic Community College
   Mays Landing, NJ 08330

Burlington County College
   Pemberton, NJ 08068

Mercer County Community College
   Trenton, NJ 08690

Union County College
   Crawford, NJ 07882

New Mexico

Eastern New Mexico University—Clovis
   Clovis, MN 88101

Eastern New Mexico University—Roswell
   Roswell, NM 88202

New Mexico State University—Carlsbad
   Carlsbad, NM 88220

Northern New Mexico Community College
El Rito, NM 87530

New York

Adirondack Community College
Queensburg, NY 12804

Corning Community College
Corning, NY 14830

Orange County Community College
Middletown, NY 10940

Suffolk County Community College
Selden, NY 11784

North Carolina

Asheville-Buncombe Technical Community College
Ashville, NC 28801

Catawba Valley Community College
Hickory, NC 28602

Central Piedmont Community College
Charlotte, NC 28235

Forsyth Technical Community College
Winston-Salem, NC 27103

Isothermal Community College
Spindale, NC 28160

Lenoir Community College
    Kinston, NC 28502

McDowell Technical Community College
    Marion, NC 28752

Sandhills Community College
    Pinehurst, NC 28374

Surry Community College
    Dobson, NC 27017

Wilkes Community College
    Wilkesboro, NC 28697

Ohio

Columbus State Community College
    Columbus, OH 43216

Cuyahoga Community College
    Cleveland, OH 44115

Edison State Community College
    Piqua, OH 45356

Lakeland Community College
    Mentor, OH 44060

Stark Technical College
    Canton, OH 44720

Washington Technical College
    Marietta, OH 45750

Oklahoma

El Reno Junior College
  El Reno, OK 73036

Northeastern Oklahoma Agricultural and Mechanical
    College
  Miami, OK 74354

Rose State College
  Midwest City, OK 73110

Tulsa Junior College
  Tulsa, OK 74119

Oregon

Central Oregon Community College
  Bend, OR 97701

Chemeketa Community College
  Salem, OR 97309

Clatsop Community College
  Astoria, OR 97103

Linn-Benton Community College
  Albany, OR 97321

Mount Hood Community College
  Gresham, OR 97030

Portland Community College
  Portland, OR 97280

Rogue Community College
  Grants Pass, OR 97527

Southwestern Oregon Community College
  Coos Bay, OR 97420

Treasure Valley Community College
  Ontario, OR 97914

Pennsylvania

Butler County Community College
  Butler, PA 16003

Community College of Allegheny County—
    Boyce
  Monroeville, PA 15146

Community College of Allegheny County—
    North
  Pittsburgh, PA 15237

Community College of Allegheny County—
    South
  West Mifflin, PA 15122

Community College of Beaver County
  Monaca, PA 15061

Harrisburg Area Community College
  Harrisburg, PA 17110

Lehigh County Community College
  Schnecksville, PA 18078

Westmoreland County Community College
Youngwood, PA 15697

South Carolina

Aiken Technical College
Aiken, SC 29802

Central Carolina Technical College
Sumter, SC 29150

Denmark Technical College
Denmark, SC 29042

Greenville Technical College
Greenville, SC 29606

Florence Darlington Technical College
Florence, SC 29501

Horry-Georgetown Technical College
Conway, SC 29528

Piedmont Technical College
Greenwood, SC 29648

Spartanburg Technical College
Spartanburg, SC 29305

Tri-County Technical College
Pendleton, SC 29670

Trident Technical College
Charleston, SC 29423

Tennessee

Cleveland State Community College
  Cleveland, TN 37320

Jackson State Community College
  Jackson, TN 38301

Nashville State Technical Institute
  Nashville, TN 37209

Northeast State Technical Community College
  Blountville, TN 37617

State Technical Institute at Memphis
  Memphis, TN 38134

Walters State Community College
  Morristown, TN 37813

Texas

Angelina College
  Lufkin, TX 75902

El Paso Community College
  El Paso, TX 79998

Grayson County College
  Denison, TX 75020

Houston Community College System
  Houston, TX 77270

Kilgore College
  Kilgore, TX 75662

Laredo Community College
  Laredo, TX 78040

Midland College
  Midland, TX 79701

Odessa College
  Odessa, TX 79762

Richland College
  Dallas, TX 75243

South Plains College
  Levelland, TX 79336

Tarrant County Junior College
  Fort Worth, TX 76102

Texas Southmost College
  Brownsville, TX 78520

Utah

Salt Lake Community College
  Salt Lake City, UT 84130

Utah Valley State College
  Orem, UT 84058

Virginia

Central Virginia Community College
Lynchburg, VA 24502

Dabney S. Lancaster Community College
Clifton Forge, VA 24422

John Tyler Community College
Chester, VA 23831

Lord Fairfax Community College
Middletown, VA 22645

Mountain Empire Community College
Big Stone Gap, VA 24219

New River Community College
Dublin, VA 24084

Northern Virginia Community College
Annandale, VA 22003

Patrick Henry Community College
Martinsville, VA 24112

Southside Virginia Community College
Alberta, VA 23821

Southwest Virginia Community College
Richlands, VA 24641

Thomas Nelson Community College
Hampton, VA 23670

Tidewater Community College
  Portsmouth, VA 23510

Wytheville Community College
  Wytheville, VA 24382

Washington

Centralia College
  Centralia, WA 98531

Clark Community College
  Vancouver, WA 98663

Columbia Basin Community College
  Pasco, WA 99301

Edmonds Community College
  Lynnwood, WA 98036

Pierce College
  Tacoma, WA 98498

Skagit Valley College
  Mount Vernon, WA 98273

Spokane Community College
  Spokane, WA 99207

Walla Walla Community College
  Walla Walla, WA 99362

West Virginia

West Virginia Northern Community College
  Wheeling, WV 26003

West Virginia University at Parkersburg
  Parkersburg, WV 26101

Wisconsin

Black Hawk Technical College
  Janesville, WI 53547

Gateway Technical College
  Kenosha, WI 53141

Madison Area Technical College
  Madison, WI 53714

Northeast Wisconsin Technical College
  Green Bay, WI 54307

Wyoming

Casper College
  Casper, WY 82601

Central Wyoming College
  Riverton, WY 82501